KALALOCH

A STATE OF MIND

BY

Vickie W. Striegel

DEDICATION

To Marian Becker Dickinson - The Soul of Kalaloch. Thank you.
To Floyd Dickinson - The Spirit of Kalaloch. Thank you.
To Dennis Striegel - The Spirit of my Soul. Thank you.

Automated Graphic Systems, Inc.
4590 Graphics Drive
White Plains, MD 20695

Library of Congress Cataloging-in-Publication Number 98-91032

Striegel, Vickie W.
        Kalaloch : A State of Mind

ISBN 0-9668572-0-8

TABLE OF CONTENTS

ACKNOWLEDGMENTS

I will be eternally grateful to all those who gave me encouragement, support, and information towards the publication of this book.

First, I must thank Marian Becker Dickinson and her wonderful husband Floyd Dickinson. If it hadn't been for them, this book would not be. They opened their home and hearts to me and were willing to share their vast knowledge and love of Kalaloch. The majority of photo's herein, came from Marian's photo albums.

The chapter on Ruby Beach would not have been possible if it hadn't been for Missy Barlow. Mrs. Barlow is a candid lady with a quick wit and earthiness that shines from crystal blue eyes. The hours we spent in her artist's studio were delightful.

To Micki Rasmussen who provided newspaper clippings, photos, and a lot of first hand knowledge about Kalaloch where she's been employed for almost twenty years, thank you. Micki was instrumental in introducing me to Marian, as well as a never ending source of encouragement when needed. And to Sam Claude who said, "Go for it." Thank you both.

Thanks to Ariele Huff, who edited my rambling prose, and to DeWane Skinner my computer guru, who both made my life a lot easier.

Many thanks to Jim Schultz, Concession Coordinator for Olympic National Park, who opened many doors within the park service. Thanks also to Mike Smithson, Chief Park Naturalist and Mike Gurling, Western District Interpreter, both of Olympic National Park, who took time out of their busy schedules to help keep me on track.

Susan Oliver, Olympic National Park historian, provided the photo of the original Kalaloch Store and the one of Ruby Beach Lodge. I owe her a great deal. (Until I'd received the Ruby Beach Lodge photo, I was unaware Ruby Beach even had a "lodge.")

Thanks to Susan Goff, Archivist of the Forks Timber Museum, who provided the article on the "Gold Mining" scam at Ruby Beach, and to Rod Fleck, Editor of *Wreckage,* a peninsula publication, and his group who do historical research on shipwrecks off the Washington coast.

Further, I would be remiss if I didn't give a heartfelt thanks to the people of Forks, Washington. The librarians at the Forks Library helped immensely in both time and information, and everyone I talked to had either information or names of people who could further this project. To Mrs. Dale Bierce who supplied her remembrances of the area, thank you.

Most importantly, I must thank my husband who put up with all my shenanigans in gathering information and photos, and taking what seemed like endless road trips hither and yon.

PHOTO CREDITS:

Jones Photography located at 1918 Simpson Avenue, Aberdeen, Washington gave special permission to use many of their photos that at one time or another graced the gift shop as postcards.

James and Gloria Ball, two of Kalaloch's most ardent fans, and two very special people, let me search through stacks of photographs they have taken over their twenty five years plus, of visiting Kalaloch and said, "Use anything you want."

Skip Smith of Smith/Western, Inc. was generous in giving permission to use many of the old "Ellis" postcard pictures.

Thank you, one and all.

The poem, "The House By The Sea" used by permission of Marian Becker Dickinson.

VS   September, 1998

FOREWORD

After my husband Dennis and I started working at Kalaloch Lodge, it soon became evident that guests wanted information about the early years of Kalaloch, but, frustratingly, there was no written history of the area.

This volume has been written to answer some of those questions. And, to those loyal Kalalochians who have visited the lodge and the campground over the years, if I've missed your favorite stories and people, I apologize. Let's chat. Maybe in future editions, we can squeeze them in. To those who are visiting with us for the first time: Welcome to a truly magical place.

The Olympic Mountains and Peninsula were born of cataclysm. As part of the Pacific Rim's "Ring of Fire," which includes our near neighbor, Mt. Rainier, a cataclysm could again alter this small corner of the world — in a heartbeat.

Wind, weather, and mankind, continuously work to change the towering peaks of Mt. Olympus as they do with every other mountain range. But the coastal region of the peninsula is even more susceptible to change than the Olympics. Four daily tides ebb and flow, reshaping the fragile landscape.

For the Native American's ancestors who first called the Olympic Peninsula home, life on this last American frontier was a dubious proposition at best. Early Europeans who tried to tame this inhospitable land didn't have it much easier.

Through the years, this has changed, and now those of us who call the West Coast of Washington home can easily say, "Life is good."

A BRIEF HISTORY

Just for a moment, let's pretend you are one of earth's earliest inhabitants, and the year is around twenty-five million B.C. As long as we're pretending, we'll say your name is Xuk and that you and the little woman, Xukette, have planned to take the wee ones for a picnic at the beach. It's a few years before Kentucky Fried Mastodon Rump "to go" is available, so Xukette has packed a large sack lunch to take along. With a mastodon rump thrown over one shoulder and a few tubers tucked into a skin sack and hung from your belt, you and your happy family head for the ocean on the western edge of — *Seattle*.

"Say what? I thought we were going to the beach? Kalaloch, or Ozette, or somewhere around there."

Remember, it's twenty-five million years ago. Gills, fins, and the ability to reach depths of hundreds of fathoms[1] would be necessary to picnic at Kalaloch because in those days, beach front property was near Seattle. There was no Kalaloch, or Hoh, or Queets, not yet, and the Olympic Mountains were still under the Pacific Ocean, collecting mollusks and mud.

Then, sometime during the Tertiary period of the Oligocene Epoch (ten to twelve million years ago), a powerful eruption dramatically changed the Seattle *beach scene*. The mountain range we know today as the Olympics, was driven skyward, then hurled against the North American continent. This small cataclysm added the piece of real estate now known as the Olympic Peninsula.

Needless to say, had you been at the Seattle beach that day, you'd have had a couple of hard jolts, at least hard enough to make a bladder or two of your Yak Beer foam over. Since that cataclysm, things have settled down a bit in the heave, thrust, and hurl department. But don't

---

1 *For those of us who are nautically challenged, a "fathom" is the equivalent of six feet.*

1

start feeling too secure, geologically speaking, the ground we trod on the Olympic Peninsula is far from grinding to a complete halt.

According to those who study that kind of thing, (mountains moving and all that stuff), a number of geologists have determined that the Olympic Mountains are still rising, and at the fastest rate of any mountains in the world.

Then, in the not too distant past, around 25,000 years ago, a small ice-sheet covered Seattle and the Puget Sound area to a depth of about three thousand feet. Not exactly a picnicker's paradise.

With all the water tied up in ice floes, the Pacific Ocean was three to four hundred feet lower than it is today. This created a dry, narrow corridor, known as the Bering Land-Bridge, or Beringa,[2] that allowed foot travel between Alaska and Siberia. The theory of this land-bridge, whether there was one or not, is further complicated by disagreement as to who, if anyone, traveled across it, and in which direction they were headed. Did they travel south from Siberia to picnic in warmer climes? Or were they headed north in quest of a careless mastodon?

Whichever direction the picnickers chose, they picnicked for too long if they intended to return, because sometime around 12,000 years ago, the climate warmed considerably. All the sea water that had been frozen in glacier form began to melt, and as the glaciers melted, the oceans rose and the Bearing Land-Bridge was engulfed. All that remains now is a thirty-six mile gap between Siberia and Alaska filled with some rather frigid water.

As late as 12,000 years ago Seattle was still buried under ice, but the thaw was on and Xuk's descendants were still feasting on mastodon meat right here on the Olympic Peninsula.

"Pshaw," you say? Well, mastodon bones, dated to around 13,000 years ago were found at the Manis Mastodon Site in Sequim in 1977.

Other things were happening on the peninsula too, though "peninsula" is a bit of a misnomer. As the ice melted, low-lying areas around Puget Sound filled with ice water and for a time, before the Strait of Juan de Fuca began to flow westward into the Pacific, the peninsula was an island. Then, as the waters of the Sound ebbed and flowed, they reached a level nearer to those we see today, and the Olympic Peninsula was born.

The waterways of yore may have been similar to those we see today, but the landscape was a different story. The giant western red cedars, Sitka spruce, and Douglas firs, were all seedlets awaiting the right conditions to sprout. Many of the land mammals unique to the Olympics were cut-off from the rest of the world and to this day some are found *only* on the peninsula.

Archaeologists have found remnants of a human culture that lived on the edges of the peninsula around twelve thousand years ago. But, from around ten thousand years ago to twenty-five hundred years ago, there's a slight gap, archaeologically speaking. Archaeologists and geologists and all of the other "ologists" can't seem to find many clues as to what was happening on the edge of the peninsula. The biggest obstacle to surmount has been the ocean's tendency to reclaim things near it's edges and to deep-six them.

Around the year 2,000 B.C., give or take a decade, the forefathers of today's Makah Indians settled around the area we call Cape Flattery and Neah Bay. Farther south at Cape Alava in 1970, a fierce Pacific storm uncovered the most significant archaeological find to date: An Ozette Indian village, buried beneath a mudslide some 450 years ago, was discovered after heavy rains washed away part of an embankment. The significance of this find is immeasurable because most of the village was still intact and allowed us a peek into the lives of the inhabitants.[3]

---

2 *Beringa was named in honor of Vitus Bering, but not all scientists agree there was a land-bridge.*

3 *Most of the artifacts recovered are on display at Neah Bay in the Makah Indian Museum. This museum is a must see while on the peninsula.*

Other than the peek the Ozette find gave us, events on the peninsula, from about 2,000 B.C. to around 250 years ago, still are the focus of a good deal of speculation with only sparse facts to suggest real answers.

It *is* known that early in the eighteenth century, the Spanish, the British, and the Americans were all frantically searching for the fabled Strait of Anan. The Strait of Anan was a storied waterway that early navigators assumed cut through the heart of the North American continent from coast to coast.

The Russians threw their fur hats in the ring in search of the elusive "Northwest Passage" when Peter the Great issued the proclamation, "Any and all lands along the west coast of the continent, not actually occupied by other powers will be claimed by Russia." Well, it sounded like a good idea at the time.

The Brits, already well established in what would become the Oregon Territory, certainly weren't about to cede any land to Russia. France, busy with problems of her own on the home front, was trying to hang onto a piece of real estate dubbed the "Louisiana Territory," and didn't have the manpower to get involved.

However, King Ferdinand VI, of Spain, took more than a wee bit of umbrage with the Russian's plan. The Spanish weren't quite through staking claims in the *New World,* so by a royal decree of his own, King Ferdinand appointed Bruno Heceta, Captain of the frigate *Santiago,* and Lt. Juan de la Bodega y Quadra, skipper of the schooner *Sonora*, to hasten forth and lay claim to everything north of Southern California.

No one knew for sure what riches, or peril, lay in that little explored land to the north, but they'd claim it *all* and sort things out later.

On March 16th 1775, the two ships sailed out of San Blas, Mexico and headed north. Aboard Heceta's ship was an ample supply of bottles that would eventually be stuffed with land proclamations, then sealed with lead and planted ashore to let all the other *players* know, "This land is claimed in the name of his Majesty, King Ferdinand VI, and Spain."

Well, this was a business trip, not a pleasure cruise, and life aboard the ships soon became anything but fun. Having left sunny Southern California, they were soon battling squalls and cold, fierce, Pacific storms. On July 13th, the two ships rendezvoused just north of what we know today as Destruction Island.[4] Since no competitor's flag flew ashore, it is supposed that Heceta decided the beach there looked as good a place as any to plant a bottle. Plans were made to do just that the next day.

July 14, 1755, Commander Heceta, accompanied by twenty armed guards, rowed ashore becoming the first *known* white man to set foot on the coast of Washington.

In the meantime, Lt. Quadra, aboard the *Sonora,* was about a half-league[5] south, where he ordered seven sailors to row ashore and return with fresh water and fuel. The un-armed men pulled away from the mother ship using all their might to battle through the pounding surf. As they neared shore, it was soon evident that the rocks and surf were the least of their worries. Historians disagree as to whether a band of Indians were hidden in the surrounding forest, or if there were a few Indians on the beach waving the men ashore.

The outcome, however, is agreed upon by almost everyone: As the boat neared shore, a band of warriors descended upon the flailing craft, dragged it ashore, and massacred all seven men. The boat was stripped of metal fittings, destroyed, and the Indians faded back into the forest. After this encounter, the island we call Destruction, was named "Island of Sorrows." The Strait of Anan was *not* discovered.

---

4 Historians disagree as to just where this first landing took place. Some say it was not near Destruction Island, but farther south at Point Grenville. For the sake of argument, the author has chosen to use the area across from Destruction Island as it is closer to Kalaloch. Besides, there are no eyewitnesses still alive who can dispute the story.

5 For land lubbers, a league is approximately three miles.

Lt. Quadra's encounter may have been one of the first incidents that took place between coastal tribes and the ever encroaching Europeans, but it was not the only one. There are many stories of clashes between the fierce coastal tribes and the interloping Europeans, by both those who hiked into the area and those who were unluckily cast upon the shores after foundering in a shipwreck.

For those who would like to find more information about shipwrecks along the coast, or Northwest Native Americans, the librarians at both the Forks Library and the Port Angeles Library are more than helpful in pointing out where to find the information you seek.

THE ORIGINAL SETTLERS

So much has been written about Native Americans that is fictional but passed off as fact, that it is rather hard for someone trying to research the early lives of those peoples who lived in the Americas long before being "discovered."

When the first white men entered the Pacific Northwest, there were many different native tribes. And, as with every other place the Europeans decided to "make their own," they brought death and disease upon a people who were ill-prepared for survival. Many of the tribes present when Quadra and Heceta sailed these waters are no more.

It is known that before the white man began to settle the peninsula, the various native tribes traded goods with one another during peaceful times, and at other times, they warred against their neighbors. The tribes co-mingled, traded slaves, and, in general, lived according to the dictates of their various creeds for some 10,000 years.

Because of the many dialects and language differences between the tribes, there evolved a kind of "trade language" called *Chinook,* used to barter and communicate. *Chinook* was based loosely on the original Chinookian language and with the arrival of the Europeans, the language became laced with a few French words thrown in by early trappers.

Some tribes moved about with the seasons, having both temporary summer homes and permanent winter quarters. They lived off the land and the bounty of the ocean with an ingenuity born of survival. In less than one hundred years, many of those clans were eliminated from the face of the earth.

THE OZETTE:

The Ozette lived on the river and lake of the same name. Carbon-14 dating indicates that an Ozette Village, uncovered in the early 1970s, was occupied from as long as 1,500 to 2,000 years ago.

The Ozettes were known as whalers, and they traded whale oil and dried fish with the Chalets for dentalia shells and blankets, which in turn were traded to the natives of Vancouver Island.

In the 1970s, the ancient village, Usaahluth, was excavated; many of the unearthed artifacts are thought to have been used in hunting and processing game. Several of the site's houses were buried by mud slides five to eight hundred years ago, and there is evidence of several later slides. After each slide, the village was once again occupied.

The population fluctuated dramatically, and in 1914 there were only seventeen people living in the Ozette Village. Many returned to Neah Bay from whence they'd fled to escape the influence of whites, and by 1937 there was only one Ozette reported living on the reservation.

Besides the Ozettes who called the area from Queets to Cape Flattery "home," there were the Queets, Hoh, Quileute, and Makahs.

THE QUEETS:

The Queets Tribe (also called Quaitsos) live around the river named after them. At times, the Queets and Quinaults, their southern neighbors, didn't exactly see eye-to-eye. At other times, especially when it came to be a matter of "safety in numbers," the tribes banded together in forays against the Clallams, Makahs, Ozettes, and Satsops.

Centrally located along the coast, the Queets often traded with other natives, both those to the north and south of them. Today's descendants live mainly in Queets and Taholah.

THE HOH:

The Hoh are known for their skill in making and using dugout canoes on both river and ocean. At one time, together with the Queets, the Hohs controlled the hunting grounds of the area. Today, most members live on and around their reservation, a 443 acre tract of land on the Pacific Coast where many of the tribe still depend on fishing for their income.

THE QUILEUTE:

Tribal belief says the Quileute (Quillayute) are descended from wolves by Dokibatt the Changer. There were six Quileute societies: The Fisherman, the Whale Hunter, the Elk Hunter, the Weather Predictor, the Medicine Man, and the Warrior. The tribesmen were proficient seal and whale hunters.

When attacked by larger tribes, they took refuge on James Island, and the Island still plays an important role in their lives.

Like most other Coastal tribes, at times there was conflict with their neighbors, and, by the same token, at times they traded goods with the same people. From the Makahs and Ozettes, they obtained goods such as dentalia and Hudson's Bay Company blankets that were in turn traded to the Quinaults for their highly prized salmon.

Also, like many of the coastal tribes, they had Potlatch ceremonies where a man's wealth was not measured by his possessions, but by what he gave away. Today the largest numbers of the Quileute live at La Push.

THE MAKAH:

We've all heard the expression, "A man's man." The Makah could be considered the "whaler's whaler." They were so skilled with canoes they could paddle far out into the Pacific in search of a mammal that made even the largest dugout seem small. According to tribal custom, the returning hunters, and the whale itself were greeted with great ritual and ceremony. Today, a large part of Makah economy centers around commercial fishing.

THE EARLY YEARS

By the late 1800s, the states east of the Mississippi were becoming settled and prosperous. Even the Wild West was fading into domesticity. The Olympic Peninsula, on the other hand, was still largely unsettled and unexplored, and aside from Alaska, the Peninsula was truly America's last frontier. And, as last frontiers go, Kalaloch was as close to the "last" of the last frontiers as you can get. As late as the 1920s, parts of the interior on the west side of the peninsula had not been explored, charted, or even come close to being populated.

From Seattle it was a mere hop-skip-and-a-rowboat to explore Port Townsend and Port Angeles in the northern reaches. Exploration of the southern portion of the state was a little tougher; folks had to figure out how to either cross or get around, the mighty Columbia River. As for those hardy souls who ventured past the comforts of Port Angeles on the north or Gray's Harbor on the south, travel was arduous at best and accomplished in one of two ways: Paddle power or flex of foot.

Some settlers braved the ocean route and took a chance by running open canoes in the ocean to the mouth of a river. Once into the mouth of the river, they "poled" up river as far as their muscle and cleverness could take them. River areas such as the Hoh, Queets, and Quillayute were first settled this way.

Poling up a river was risky business at best, and more than one river-runner lost hard-earned supplies to rapid water and hidden tree limbs. The unfortunate ones ended up taking a chilly bath in river water running straight off the glaciers of Mount Olympus.

The other mode of travel, by foot, was along trails originally stamped out of the forests by wild game, Indians, and an occasional trapper. You may think that foot travel would be easier and a whole bunch safer than traveling by canoe. You'd be wrong. Foot travel was not without its perils. A trek from Port Angeles to the ocean was never undertaken lightly.

In his autobiography, *Footprints in The Olympics,* early settler Chris Morganroth described his first journey to the Bogachiel River: He and a companion were put ashore at Physt where they had to wade through ankle deep mud and water for a quarter of a mile to the mainland. Once they gained firm footing, they slogged through a few cedar swamps[6] to the cabin of one of the first settlers. There, they were warned by the local that there was no water for some sixteen miles ahead. So, they stocked up on the precious fluid and, with seventy-five pound packs on their backs, headed into a great unknown. It didn't take them long to realize that the gentleman's warning about no water was just a bit *WRONG!* They forded a "fresh water" river *fourteen times* in a relatively short distance.

Should you ever doubt the hardiness and stamina of those who first explored the peninsula's interior, take a stroll across the street from the Kalaloch campground and try to bushwhack your way through a healthy stretch of undergrowth. It'll give you a whole new respect for brambles, slippery tree trunks, and slugs. If you make it a hundred feet, times the effort by sixty miles and throw in a seventy-five pound backpack for good measure. If that doesn't torque your crank, try it in the rain—without Gortex.

Or, if you're really into challenges, try it like the "Iron Man of the Hoh," John Huelsdonk, did—with a cast iron stove strapped to your back. When asked if it had been a hard trip, he replied that the only time he had trouble was when the hundred pound sack of flour in the oven shifted.

C.A. Gilman and his son S.C. explored much of the interior of the "west end" and pronounced it to be, "excellent farm land." They further predicted that in a few short years, hoards of settlers would be flocking to the area. The Gilman's were wrong on both counts.

The only cleared farmland was that near river bottoms. If spring plowing under water laden with tree trunks and flotsam galore doesn't bother you, the thought that this area receives 140 inches plus of rain a year should. Clearing land away from the rivers was not an easy answer either. The size of the trees and lack of adequate equipment for removal were the greatest deterrents. If young George Washington had lived on the Olympic Peninsula, Dad never would have had to worry about his son cutting down his trees. When a tree measures eleven feet across, it takes a bit more than a wee lad with a dull ax to fell it.

Most who settled on the peninsula in the early days didn't settle for long. The hardships on families were dramatic. It wasn't like you could go to the corner store on a whim for a loaf of bread and gallon of milk. Even if you could, cash-in-hand was not an easy-to-come-by commodity. Of those who stayed, men often had to leave their families to fend for themselves for part of the year, while they worked elsewhere to earn money to buy needed supplies.

There were, however, those who made a go of it. Most started with a small family garden and a "make-do" cabin. Gradually, a permanent home, barn, and other buildings were added, but even with these *luxuries,* life was far from easy. Those who left to seek more hospitable climes left a myriad of abandoned structures behind, most of which have long since returned to the soil and forest. Some abandoned structures remained to be reclaimed by new adventurers, but most did not. The soil was poor or swampy, the "boom" never materialized, and the solitude was unbearable for all but a few hardy souls.

During the late 1890s, settlers began homesteading along the mouths of the major rivers— the Hoh, Quillayute, and Queets. Even along smaller creeks running into the Pacific people were beginning to set up housekeeping. Possible railroad routes were surveyed on both the east side

6 *Western red cedar grew to gigantic proportions in the wet climate of the peninsula, and it loves swampy ground.*

and west end of the peninsula, and the talk of a railroad raised the hopes of many settlers, but the "talk" never came to fruition.

Of those homesteaders who stayed, the ultimate goal was to "prove up" on their land. To "prove up" they had to meet certain requirements set forth by the government such as plowing and planting a specific number of acres in a certain number of years. A small home, usually a log cabin was erected first, and for those serious about staying, outer buildings were added later. A family garden was also one of the first tasks undertaken. Most settlements had a variety of farm animals to add variety to their meager diets and to help with the work: a few milk cows, pigs, a horse or two, chickens, and occasionally sheep.

The deprivations these first settlers endured was epic, and to keep in touch with their nearest neighbors, one of the families often donated land for either a church, a school, or both.

Much depended on how "stable" the settler's life was This stability often dictated the size of the home, and more often the size of the barn. If the resident was around for any length of time, additional structures were eventually erected such as a chicken coop, root cellar, even a saw mill.

In reality, it was a rough and spartan life those first settlers faced. Frills were for city folks, and when one has to pack-in *all* the necessities of life on one's back or struggle to "pole" it up-stream against a swift current, one tends to reconsider exactly what constitutes necessity.

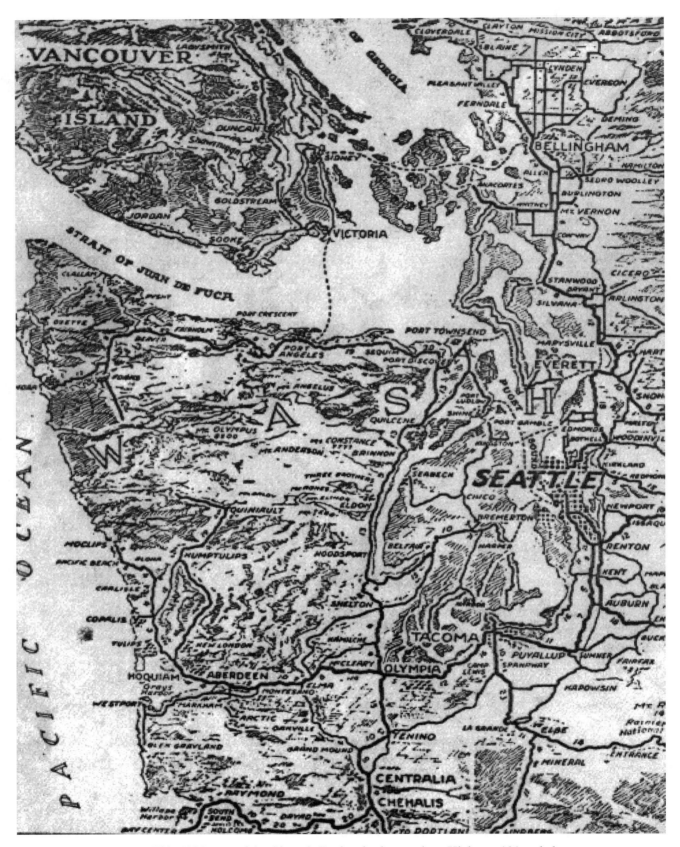

This 1925 map of the Olympic Peninsula shows where Highway 101 ended.

THE LEGACY BEGINS

In the late 1890s, Tom Lawler, who had been a building contractor in Aberdeen, built a cabin and a cannery on the north side of Kalaloch Creek near its mouth.

The old cannery sat on the small tip of land across the creek from Kalaloch Lodge. Clams, and crab were processed.

The first homes along Kalaloch Creek. Charlie Becker and family lived in one of these structures when they first moved to Kalaloch before other accomodations were built.

Around the same time, and also near the creek, Samuel R. Castile built a split board and shake home. By 1903 a post office was doing business out of the Castile home and a few others had staked out home sites in the area. The name the families gave their "city" was Castile, and by 1907 the population had swelled to seventeen.

By 1922, the name Kalaloch had replaced Castile, and not only was there a post office, but also a school. The school was part of the Clearwater School District, and class was held in the "schoolmarm's" bedroom, which just happened to be upstairs in the Lawler home.

The teacher, J[o]an Bochinski, was in her first year of teaching and boarded with the

This 1921-22 school record shows the two pupils enrolled in Miss Bochinski's class, although Jack Thompson's record shows no sign of his presence.

Lawler family. The Lawler's adopted daughter, Grace, was Miss Bochinski's sole student, even though the records show two students enrolled.

The class room consisted of one desk, one seat, and a kitchen chair used as the teacher's seat. A piece of black painted plywood was used as a blackboard, and in the winter months, warmth came from a metal stovepipe that ran upstairs from a heater below. There were no curtains or floor coverings, and Miss Bochinski told of a glorious view out her bedroom window, where she liked to while away her hours watching life in the "meadow" across the creek.

Then, in 1924, one of Kalaloch's landowners, Mr. George Northrup, declared that if and when a permanent highway should be laid across this virgin land, it would undoubtedly be placed alongside the Clearwater River.

Going with the flow, so to speak, he sold his acreage at Kalaloch and moved southeast to the Clearwater and his forecasted highway. The purchaser of this seaside, roadless tract of land was Mr. Charles W. Becker, Sr. and family.

Charlie Becker had moved from California to Hoquiam, Washington where he established a bicycle shop. Sometime there-after, he opened one of the first automobile dealerships in the Grays Harbor area. Then, he was told by physicians in Aberdeen and Hoquiam that his time here on earth was short. "Bad ticker," they told him. He was in his fifties.

Charlie Becker and friends outside his bicycle shop in Hoquiam.

So, Mr. Becker, a devout fisherman, and one who had been fishing at Kalaloch, cast one eye upon what looked to be a prime fishing "hole," and the other eye towards a hunch that the

Charles W. Becker

highway would run past Kalaloch rather than up along the Clearwater. And, just in case any of you doubt the merits of fishing, Mr. Becker lived until he was eighty-three years old.

Once Mr. Becker had acquired the forty acres on the south side of Kalaloch Creek, he realized one cannot totally support a family by reeling in steel-head and digging clams.

The family was living in an old house that had been left by a previous owner, and over the next few years (until the road came through in 1931), he and his son Bill laid claim to lumber salvaged from the beach and constructed a small store and a few modest cabins. After the store

From top: A bridge under construction during the building of Highway 101. People came to Kalaloch
anyway they could. The unpaved road was rough on automobiles, and some enthusiasts
risked a beach landing. The original Becker's Inn with some of the crew.

was built, the post office was moved into it, and the Becker's hung out their shingle. Becker's Cabin Camp was in business.

The first cabins built were called "semi-modern" cabins, and numbered one through nine. Later, five "modern" cabins were added. The semi-modern cabins had no bathroom facilities, so folks had to use an ablution block located near where today's "Seacrest" motel unit stands. The ablution block had showers and restroom facilities, and several people have told me they used to sneak up the beach trail to take a shower when life at the campground got a bit ripe.

Heat was provided by wood stoves that were later converted to kerosene, and then LP (liquid propane) stoves were added. The cabins were rustic, but the one thing the Becker's insisted on was that every bed had a good, quality mattress. The princely sum for all this tender loving care: $2 per night for a semi-modern cabin and $4 for a modern cabin. How times change.

The original Inn top, cabins and store on the right and an aerial view from the 1940's.

In the mid-thirties, the original main Inn was built, and the name was changed to Becker's Ocean Resort.[7] The new "Inn" included four lodge rooms and one bathroom upstairs; downstairs was a kitchen, a two-table dining room, and twelve stools placed around a "U"-shaped counter. (This building was in the same location as the present day Kalaloch Lodge.)

7 The name "Kalaloch Beach Ocean Village" and "Kalaloch Lodge" weren't used until after the park service took the facilities over.

With no permanent roads along the beach area in 1925, anyone desiring a little R&R had to desire it enough to make the arduous journey to Kalaloch. A journey for the faint of heart it was not.

To get to Kalaloch from the south required a trip by boat from Hoquiam to Minards, which was near Ocean Shores. Then it was a choice of backpack or horseback for the next leg of the journey to Quinault. Crossing the Quinault River was accomplished via Indian canoe, and once you were on the north side of the stream, it was thirty or so miles more to the Queets River. At the Queets, there was a choice of crossings: On weekends, a cable ferry that held up to four automobiles operated, or one crossed by Indian canoe. Needless to say, this journey was not undertaken on a mere two-days-off weekend.

Those who trekked in from the north had to contend with ways to get across the Sol Duc, Calawah, and Hoh Rivers. Once past the Hoh, it was through the thicket to Kalaloch Creek. In those early days the creek was forded via a swinging bridge used by the postal service to deliver the mail. The bridge was located in the area just a bit north and east of Highway 101, and then a path led across the road to the Becker's store and cabins.

No matter how arduous the expedition, there were those with enough optimism and zest for life to make the journey. They came for beach weddings, Indian weddings, receptions, graduation parties, Christmas parties, New Years celebrations, and, not least of all, "just to get-away-from-it-all."

This photo was taken on the day Highway 101 opened. The ribbon cutting was held in front of the store.

In the end, Mr. Northrup's prediction (luckily) missed its mark. The foretold highway did not go up along the Clearwater River. In August of 1931, a ceremonial ribbon-cutting heralded a new era on the Olympic Peninsula; Highway 101 was complete and officially open for traffic...traffic that flowed right past Kalaloch.

The ribbon-cutting ceremony was held right in front of Kalaloch's Store, and Governor Roland Hartly as well as numerous locals and state officials attended the ceremony.

The most distinguished guest on Highway 101 visited the Olympic Peninsula in 1937. President Franklin Delano Roosevelt (the second Roosevelt to visit the Olympics) and his chauffeur, took a grand tour of the park. Rumor has it that they filled the gas tank of their open touring car at Kalaloch's gas pumps.

The new highway followed a path fairly close to the original trails, and those who had persevered in their solitary lives were soon joined by hoards of fun seekers in automobiles. Life at Becker's Cabin Camp became a whole lot busier. Expansion of facilities was a high priority, and more cabins were added between 1934 and 1936.

The first communications with the outside world were via an old wall-crank telephone, and power was provided by a Whitney, diesel-powered engine. *Real* power didn't come to Kalaloch until 1969 when public power lines strung from Aberdeen finally reached the area.

Sometime before the ribbon cutting ceremonies, Charlie Becker traded an acre of ground to a Mr. Nixon in exchange for help in clearing ground for more cabins. Nixon's piece of real

Originally Nixon's Inn, this house became the Ultiken place.

estate was on the east side of the road in the area where today's employees are housed, and became known as Nixon's Inn. Like the Beckers, Nixon's Inn offered lodging and meals. Eventually, Mr. Nixon sold his land and the house he'd built upon it to Dick Ultiken who used it as a family home rather than an inn.

The Murrow Place. Owned by Edward R. Murrow's family.

Murrow's Garden   *An old tractor helped with the garden chores.*

Charlie sold another acre of property at the far southern end of Becker's to his brother Fred who built five small cabins on his land: cabin numbers 16, 17, 18, 19, and 20. Fred had a wood shed back there also. Well, Fred wasn't supposed to sell the property, but he did. He sold it to the family of Edward R. Murrow—America's star war reporter.

Murrow's folks lived in cabin sixteen, and during those early years, they planted a wonderful garden with much of the produce used by the inn for guests' meals in the dining room.

Without a doubt, the best thing to come down the new Highway 101 was a wisp of a girl named Marian Sechrist. Marian and her friend Flossy, were hired by Bill Becker as waitress/servers around 1939.

Two years after Marian began her career as a waitress, she and Bill were married. Marian's gift for remembering names and her ability to make one and all feel welcome and at "home," and Bill's shrewd business savvy made Becker's a booming haven for vacationers. Families, singles, couples, young, and old were all treated warmly like old and trusted friends which many of them were.

Then, in 1940, President Roosevelt signed into life a bill that would forever change the lives of all who lived along the northwest coast of Washington, especially those living between Ruby Beach and Kalaloch.

The decision, made by the powers that were and pushed through Congress by Harold Ickes, Secretary of the Interior, was for a narrow strip of land along the coast to be included in Olympic National Park. The area, approximately one mile wide at its widest, extended from Shi Shi Beach at the northern end to three miles above the Queets River on the southern end. This preemption of land brought down the final curtain on a bevy of budding autocamps that had sprung up along the coast. Becker's was the exception.

Some of the would-have-been entrepreneurs were given the opportunity of staying on with a year-to-year lease of "their" property. Most opted out. Becker's was saved from the same demise by the ability of Bill Becker to bargain with the "powers that were."

Marian and Flossy in their waitress uniforms.

Bill & Marian Becker

Mr. and Mrs. Becker and Art Hoover (local Handyman) August 1941

Clockwise from Top Left:

Old Nick, The Cook with Marian & Flossy;
The Dinning Room in the Original Lodge;
The First Employee Housing;
Marian Becker with her Mother, Mrs. Sechrist;
Mrs. Charlie Becker;
Art (a local) Graced the front of the store;
Old Nick, The Cook.

An areial view of the origianl lodge, store and cabin lay out.

The original Becker's Inn, store, and some of the first cabins.

Pictures Left to Right, Top to Bottom.
Original cabins 1 through 8
None of these cabins exist today.

Cabin 9

Cabin 10 (1964)

Cabin 10 (1984)

The second cabin 12 was constructed in 1964 and removed in 1984.
Note the water tower on the left hand side of the photo.

The original cabin 12 was clasified as a "modern" cabin because it had indoor plumbing.
This cabin was removed sometime prior to 1964.

Picure page 25; Areal Photograph of Kalaloch 1941
Picture page 26; Elephant Rock near Queets River.

THEN CAME THE WAR

In 1941 the United States was in the throes of World War II, and the Armed Forces (first the Army Signal Corp. and later the Coast Guard) "landed" at Becker's. With the bombing of Pearl Harbor, it was determined that one of the most vulnerable places on U.S. soil was the West Coast of America.

Indeed, the threat to the West Coast was not without merit. Not only was a Japanese submarine spotted off the coast, but the Japanese had discovered what would become known as the Japanese Current. This current flows much like a giant river within the ocean and affects the flow of the Pacific as well as the air currents above.

The Japanese designed balloons, big balloons, balloons that measured thirty-five feet in diameter. The balloons in themselves were not harmful; the fact they were equipped with twenty-five to sixty pounds of incendiary bombs made them lethal. The balloon bombs were set adrift on the air currents from Honshu, one of Japan's northern islands.

It's estimated that 9,300 of these "airborne surprises" caught the prevailing winds and headed for the U.S. Coast. Ultimately, not all of them made it, but there were balloons found as far east as Michigan. Others showed up in Mexico, Canada, Alaska, and Hawaii with the Western states of Washington, Oregon, California, and Montana receiving the largest share.

Two of the devices were recovered from the Olympic Peninsula, one at Vaughn (now known as Gig Harbor) and the other at Chimacum.

Of all the balloon-bombs that made it to the shores of the United States, the most devastating was found by a group of children who were on a picnic with the local reverend's wife. It is assumed that one of the children hit the bomb with a rock, and all five people died instantly—the only war-related deaths of Americans on U.S. soil during the war.

When Kalaloch was taken over by the Armed Forces, Becker's Inn was commandeered as head-quarters, and fun-loving beach bums were replaced by men in uniform with "war dogs" that patrolled the beaches. Even Bill Becker did his part as a member of the Coast Guard at Kalaloch. With his knowledge of the area, he was a valuable recruit.

All of Becker's Cabin Camp was considered the "base" for the service-men except for cabin 15. Cabin 15 had a couple of double beds, a small kitchen, and a bathroom. Bill, Marian, and family were housed in it.

Coastguardsmen Patroling Kalaloch during world war II

With gas rations in effect, travel for pleasure was pretty much out of the picture, and business at the resort was somewhere between zero and nil.

During the military occupation, there were blackouts and alerts-most of which never came to fruition, but Marian recalled one instance when the alert was real:

"A coastguardsman came to me and told me to go right away with the baby, take whatever food and clothes I could carry, and get lost in the woods. I went back on the swinging bridge over Kalaloch Creek and hiked back into the woods for two hours. I was really frightened and tired and had no idea where Bill was. A while later, a coastguardsman found me and told me the alert was over. I was sure glad to get back home."

That alert wasn't the only excitement the Beckers had. In March of 1944, a plane landed on the beach just south of Kalaloch Creek. It was low tide, and a plane landing so close created quite a stir. It wasn't long before several loggers hauled their equipment down to the beach to help pull the plane farther up on the beach and away from the high-tide line. Two men in parkas climbed out of the plane and refused to let anyone near it. Apparently, the plane had something to do with a top-secret mission. They'd taken off from Alaska, and when they ran out of gas (or had mechanical problems), the beach became a landing strip.

The plane sat where it had landed and remained under guard while the daily tides immersed it over and over. A few days later, trucks came out and air force personnel took the plane apart piece by piece and carried it away.

Glenn Barkhurst, who was stationed at the base during the plane incident, took photos of the downed craft, but even he wasn't allowed to go near it. Fifty year's later at a National Park function for "old timers," Mr. Barkhurst presented those photos to Marian. He told her he'd researched the air force archives, and there was never a mention of this plane--anywhere.

The Mystery Plane March 27, 1944 Second day on the beach.

During the Coast Guard's occupancy of the Inn, someone got careless and didn't pay much attention to the old stove in the kitchen. The hood over the stove was made of wood, wood that grease had been allowed to build up on, a volatile combination. From her temporary home in cabin 15, Marian Becker watched her quaint, once comfortable inn go up in smoke.

A hastily Built Mess Hall replaced the original lodge that burned down.

The inn was gone, but the Coast Guard wasn't, and a mess hall was hastily constructed where the present-day Kalaloch Lodge now stands. The Coast Guard made-do with the mess hall, and at the end of the war, the troops moved on and the Beckers moved into the mess hall.

The Beckers weren't the only folks along the coastal area affected by the war. Alice Bierce, wife of Dale Bierce, was kind enough to share her memories of the time she and her family lived at Ruby Beach while her husband was stationed there with a radar unit during the war:

"...The Radar Unit was set up out on the point of land westward from the Kalalock Lodge. It was not an operating lodge then. There were only Indians (mostly Hoh) plus a few loggers who weren't drafted besides the group of Army men who ran and repaired the Radar. My husband was the chief of maintenance. The group he joined there were not trained on the Radar they gave them. So my husband was brought in from California. I can't remember how many men there were. But there was a fair sized group on the upper side of [Highway] 101 at the bend at Ruby Beach. There were several of us married (we even had our 3 year old daughter with us) who lived in the cabins a couple operated down below the road at Ruby Beach. We were right on the beach in fact we cleared out like a little park in front of us (not the huge logs way in front). The cabins were just one room with a wood stove & table & chairs. There was no refrigeration. I'd never had smelt before, but the Indians came down & netted them at the mouth of the river. They kept us supplied. We used small cans of meat & the Captains wife took 4 or 5 wives into Forks once a week. Then we got fresh meat but had to cook & use it right then. The families were invited to walk up across [Highway] 101 and have Sunday dinner with the other soldiers.

There was very little travel on the roadway. My folks saved their gas coupons & were able to come visit from our home in South Seattle. Mom & I went for a walk & she spotted wild strawberries by the road. We picked enough to make a tiny shortcake. My Dad was an ardent fisherman. He had a book about all the state's rivers. He looked up that one & we had fresh fish. The soldiers had tried & never got a thing, so Dad was busy teaching them how to fish.

My husband's best man worked at Bremerton Navy Yard. He & [his] wife came over too & we came down to Kalaloch & razor clams. She made pancakes & cut the digger in two & put it on the top side before she flipped them. Delicious!

In 1972 our daughter was on the kidney machine & very ill in Spokane. I commuted there for the eight months. The last time she was in the hospital the nurse told us we'd better get out for some R & R as things were just going to get worse. So we headed for Kalalock! First time we'd been back on the ground since VJ Day! (We'd flown around the peninsula & over to Ocean Shores for lunch). We didn't know you had to have a years reservation to come. We were amazed & terribly disappointed. The gal at the desk told us to go have a cup of coffee - they were having a discussion with a guest. Turns out it was a couple from California with their year's reservation. They were not pleased with all the rustic rooms etc. Soon the desk-gal came & said we could have that room upstairs in the Lodge. The couple headed on for Port Angeles! We just Praised the Lord!

We later went up to Ruby Beach & were amazed. All the cabins were gone. The Army Camp was all grown up with trees. There was no sign at all that we'd spent 4 or 5 months there with all the accompanying buildings etc. There had been gun emplacements up below the road south of where our cabins were. Dale walked all over looking, because he was sure he remembered where they were. They were made of cement. Never did find them.

The Radar Unit was set up to intercept the Incendiary balloons the Japanese were sending. So it was a hush-hush thing. But the secrecy had been so good Japan never knew that there had been damage, even some killed in Oregon I believe. They thought the balloons never got through. So by the time the Radar unit was set up, there had been no balloons to find! There were P38's at Payne Field by Everett who were supposed to intercept them.

One extra side-light. All along 101 between Ruby Beach & Kalalock those beaches were claimed by different families of Indians. One enterprising group built a lift up the cliff to bring the smelt. Another group asked to use it & were told "No". So the phone line along the road the Army had between the two spots, Ruby Beach and Kalalock, was ripped out - The second group, in the middle of the night, took a truck & pulled the lift out & deposited it down the road. The Army was frantic--must be sabotage--the FBI even was involved I think before they found it was just a family feud. Hope this is something you can use for background. Been 25 years in August [1997] since we came back. My son who wasn't born till 1947 (he'll be 50 in Nov.) took me over as a birthday gift. My daughter, husband, Mom & Dad are all with the Lord. Wish I'd written down their observations." [8]

The Lord bless

Bill Becker and Friend in uniform.

Lt. Bill Becker U.S. Coastguard

8 *I've taken the liberty of including Mrs. Bierce's letter as it was written to me. Her words are much more eloquent than I could have hoped to do justice to. Thank you Mrs. Bierce.*

Building the new lodge.

32

THE GOOD OLD DAYS

After the war years of gas and food rationing, it took awhile to move forward, but in 1952 a larger version of the main inn was begun. Becker's Inn was finished in 1953, and once again, the family took up residency in their "home."

The building of the new inn.

At first, part of the family lived in what is now known as "room one" in the main lodge, and Bill and Marian moved next door into "room two." Rooms one and two later became popular with guests because they had outside entrances and a view of the ocean. As business boomed, room two was converted to an additional dining area because the other dining room just wasn't large enough to handle the crowds.

After room two was made into a dining room, Marian and Bill moved into a variety of cabins, staying in each one long enough to get it refurbished before moving to the next. Then, in

The Becker's New Home.

1964 the Beckers began to build a home across the street from the lodge to help ease the crowded conditions of their growing family.

Another improvement for the resort, a motel unit was added and named "Seacrest" in honor of Marian's Dad, Merle Sechrist. Mr. Sechrist loved Kalaloch and wrote the following poem:

THE HOUSE BY THE SEA

I have lived in a house by the side of the road,
And have watched men fight for greed;
And I have fought without giving thought
As to how much was my need.

Now I'm growing tired of this roadside house,
Where I've seen so much of crime;
Where every man grabs all he can
Without regard to time.

I want to live where I can think
Of the beautiful things in life;
Where I can be with a soul so free
There would be no struggle or strife.

Let me live in a house by the side of the sea,
Instead of the one by the road;
Where the roar of the Deep will lull me to sleep,
And lighten my troublesome load.

I want it to be on a nice grassy plot,
With a bluff to keep breakers away;
And a nice sandy beach within easy reach
Where men can be boys and just play.

I want to look thru my window and gaze
At the rolling and tumbling sea;
And watch phosphorus light the breakers at night
While the moonbeams dance for me.

When the night has gone and the dawn breaks through,
And the sun takes full command;
I'll shed no tears for my worldly fears
As I play there on the sand.

So let me live in a house by the sea,
I would much rather have it than gold;
I just want to be the boy that is me
Before I grow weary and old.

Here is a view of my house by the sea,
The lawn is spacious and green;
It is built on a bluff which for me is enough,
My cabin with number fourteen.
Seacrest [Sechrist]

The building of Cabin 14.

Mr. and Mrs. Merle Sechrist.

For over half a century, the Beckers ran Becker's Cabin Camp. That's around 18,250 days worth of service. Through those years, untold numbers of meals were cooked, sheets washed, sunburns gotten, kites flown, sea shells gathered, and countless guests and employees who passed through and mixed in with the Beckers lives.

The author was fortunate enough to visit with Marian Becker Dickinson, and Marian was kind enough to share many of her family memories from those early years. She said during our visit that we would need a lifetime to cover all the events that occurred during her years at Kalaloch. I agree. Years and a tome weighing 4,000 pounds probably wouldn't even scratch the surface. So, I've included a very limited recollection of some of her favorite stories:

One of Marian's favorite employees was Barney. Barney, a large woman, worked for the Beckers for twenty-five years, and the first time Marian met her was when she entered the Kalaloch Store one cold winter day:
"When I first saw Barney, she weighed over 200 pounds. It was winter time and she had a great big fur coat on that made her look 300 pounds. It was early in the morning, and I hadn't been at Kalaloch long. I was a bride you know, 20 or so. I was the postmaster, and we

Barney in her fur coat.

Barney was third postmaster at Kalaloch.

opened a little before nine. When I opened the door, I looked as this big woman come in. She said, 'Jesus Christ, it's cold in here. Why the hell don't ya build a fire?' It was cold, and the old heater hadn't had time to warm the place up yet... ."

Starting with this somewhat inauspicious meeting, Marian and Barney became best of friends. Marian called Barney, "A diamond in the rough," because like a gem of great value, she had a few flaws but was still a priceless gem.

Another time, Marian was working in the lodge and Barney was running the store. In those days, the store employees wore "many different hats." They handled gas sales, grocery sales, reservations, and just about everything else. Marian needed change, so she went over to the store and quietly slipped in the back door. She could see a long line of people, winding all the way out the door and around, and Barney was working fast and furiously. Some folks wanted groceries, others had pumped gas, and there were those waiting to either obtain cabin reservations or check-in to rooms. Barney was fast, and it wasn't long before the line dwindled down to one little man who stood nervously before the imposing clerk. Her patience had worn thin after the rush, and Barney snapped at him, "Now what the hell do you want?"

Meekly he replied, "I'm the Reverend Lieby. And I think I have a reservation."

Barney was mortified. She'd just sworn at a reverend. She then proceeded to stumble and fumble all over the place trying to redeem herself.

The reverend, a man who practiced what he preached, quickly forgave the distraught woman, and as if to prove there were no hard feelings, the Liebys returned to Kalaloch every year to make sure Barney was behaving herself.

Marian recalled only one time in Barney's twenty-five years of service that anyone took offense at her colorful language. Shortly after the war, a couple drove up to the gas pumps in a sedan, then entered the store. Because of the gas rationing from the war years, the husband asked Barney, "How much gas can we get?"

"Deary, you can get all that you want," said Barney.

Well, the wife took offense at the word "deary," and got right up in Barney's face, "How dare you call my husband deary!" "Come on," she said grabbing her husband's hand and dragging him out the door. "We're going. We're not gonna get gas from her."

Barney with her "pimp stick"
and Marian.

Barney was also a great tease. When the loggers would come in for a cold brew after a long day in the woods, she'd always ask them, "Do your wives know you're buying beer?"

Marian confided that, "Barney was the one who taught me how to smoke." Barney would say, "Here Marian, have a pimp stick." Marian laughed and admitted, "I didn't even know what a pimp stick was."

All of us know a Barney: forthright, blunt, and to-the-point, but always with a twinkle in the eye that lets you know no matter what comes out of her mouth, you can trust her with your life. When Barney passed from this earthly plain, she was sorely missed by all. "A diamond in the rough?" Maybe. Or an angel watching over the store to this day?

And, by the way, the next time you're at Kalaloch, go into the store and notice the green paint on the floor. Marian painted it there—a long, long time ago.

As long as you're wandering around looking for bits of history, stroll on over to the gift shop in the main lodge. On the back wall of the room, above the fireplace, is a mural. The mural was painted in 1953/1954, by artist Mrs. John White. The people portrayed in the mural were all local folks, some living, some deceased. According to Marian they were:

The Trapper	Bill Becker
Fisherman	Whimpy Sampson, of Queets
Crab pot Fisherman	Bud Sailto, of Queets
Hunter	Bouley Hicks, of Raft River
Woodsman	Reil Davis, of Queets
Shakecutter	Buck Wells, of Queets
Salmon Netter	Warren Lee, of Queets
Smelt Dipper	Dusty Obi, of Queets
Indian Basket Weaver	Lilly Bell, of Queets
Tourist	Coby White (Son of Artist)
Tourist	John White (Husband of Artist)
Tourist - with beach towel	Heather White (Daughter of Artist)

Bill Becker was the consummate "PR" man. One day, three college girls from Seattle stopped by and were heartbroken when told there was, "No room at the Inn." Seeing their disappointed faces, Bill joked, "Well, if you really want to stay that bad, we'll fill the old truck with some hay, and you can sleep in the garage in the truck." The trio went for it! So, Bill told Frank, an employee, to fill the back of the truck with fresh hay and park it over in the garage for the threesome.

The next morning the women commented that it was the best night's sleep they'd ever had. After their return home, they sent the Beckers a letter:

June 9, 1938

To the Beckers and Frank:

Arrived home safely—believe it or not (guess the Lord looks after fools and drunks—you know we weren't drunk).

Have often thought of you and your kindness and want to thank you for letting us sleep with the truck—I'll bet it wouldn't go after we left. Dear Frank: Is your conscience still bothering you?

Everyone got a kick out of the picture of us taken in the garage—especially the bed-post. Please don't frame our pictures with it

We certainly had a lovely time at your place and you saved our trip from becoming a complete disappointment.

Hoping to see you soon,

THREE GALS ON A MATTRESS

Ace was another local character. He looked after the "primitive campground" north of the lodge. He also liked to look after the ladies and visit with them. One day, he watched as a couple of gals from Kansas parked down by the beach trail, got out of their car, and pulled a gallon jug out. He followed them to the top of the beach trail and watched as they made their way down to the ocean. They filled their jug with water and hiked back up.

"Whatcha got there, ladies?" he asked.

"Oh, we got this jug of ocean water to take back to Kansas," they answered.

"Well, you better pour some out 'cause when the tide comes in the jug will break," said Ace.

The girls poured some out, got back in their car, and away they went.

Many of you have looked wistfully across the waves towards Destruction Island and thought it would be a neat place to visit if you only had the means to get there. This story should interest you. One day a couple of local fellows, Rocky and Paul, asked Marian if she'd like to ride with them in a dory out to the island. She said, "Sure." On the way out, the fellows pulled up Rocky's crab pots, so they could give the crabs to the coastguardsman and his family who manned the lighthouse. Marian said every time they grabbed hold of a pot the dory would just about stand on its end.

As they worked the old dory into the island's big rocks,[9] seals, lots of seals, one-by-one dominoed out of the dory's way. When they got in there, Marian said it was the most beautiful place she'd ever seen.

After landing, the coastguardsman and his wife fed them donuts and hot coffee to warm them up, and in turn, the trio gave the man and his wife the fresh crabs. The lighthouse keeper asked if Marian would like to climb the stairs up to the light. Ever curious about what the view would be, Marian made the climb around and around and around to the top. "It was a view I'll never forget," were her words.

The guardsman asked if she'd sign the official "visitor's register," and though her hands were cold and kind of shaky, sign she did. When she had finished, she glanced at the name above hers and saw a name written in beautiful penmanship with a date from the 1800s.[10]

By the way, if you have big plans to find a way to get out to the island, cancel them. The island is part of the National Marine Sanctuary and is, therefore, off limits except by special permit.

If you stop at the turnout just north of Beach Trail 6, which is directly across from the island, you'll notice a couple of sawed-off posts sticking up on the ocean side of the guardrail. At one time, not too long ago, these posts were much taller and held a large wooden sign commemorating this area as the place where Quadra's men were set upon by the Indians. The sign was removed a few years ago—under the guise of political "correctness."

Funny thing is, a lot of folks have asked about the sign, and all they mention in relationship to it was the fact that on high-wind days, it swung straight out horizontally as the ocean breezes dictated.

9. *If you have a pair of binoculars, take them to the turn out just north of Beach Trail 6 on Highway 101. At low tide you'll see there's more to Destruction Island than meets the naked eye.*
10. *The register is now in the Clallam County Museum in the city of Port Angeles.*

Views of Destruction Island

TRIVIA FROM THE PAST

Following are some questions often asked by guests at Kalaloch, as well as some information about the area that is not well known.

WHAT'S THE ARCH FOR?

One day, a regular at Kalaloch, mentioned to Marian that something needed to be done about the towering brick fireplace on the south end of the inn. His concern was that with a structure that high, the possibility of a disaster was in the making should all those bricks come tumbling down. Marian agreed there was a potential problem, but what to do? John White, a family man who visited the resort every year told her, "I'll get the right person to put an I-beam up there as a brace." And he did. He contacted Bethlehem Steel and had an I-beam designed and shipped to Kalaloch where it was placed against the offending brickwork.

Marian took one look at the barren I-beam and got a hold of another long-time friend, Herbie Evans. "Herbie," she said, "we've got a problem. What can you do to hide that eyesore?"

Herbie had laid most of the brick in Tacoma before coming to the area, and in short order, he had that I-beam looking remarkably like the "arch" you see today.

Steel posts were placed around the I-beam, so cars, buses, and trucks wouldn't damage the structure, and Herbie solved that eyesore problem too by making planter boxes around the posts.

WHY DO OVERLY AND MACY HAVE NAMES INSTEAD OF NUMBERS?

Overly and Macy cabins were named in honor of the first two Olympic National Park Superintendents. Preston Macy was the first superintendent, and he was succeeded by Fred Overly.

Marian chose to name the two cabins after these men who were not just "park" people but personal friends of the Beckers. So, unofficially, the cabins are numbers 17 (Macy) and 18 (Overly). Officially, they're Macy and Overly, and everyone calls them that.

Mr. & Mrs. Overly

The original wooden water tower had a cranberry bog under it and provided fresh cranberries for lodge guests.

THE WATER TOWER

In the early days across the street from the lodge and behind where the generator shed of today rests, stood an old water tower. When I started this project, pictures of the tower seemed to be scarcer than hen's teeth, but Marian came through again. Not only does she have photos of one water tower, but she also has a photo of the original wooden water tower.

Today there is scant evidence that either tower ever existed. Their cross-barred legs have disappeared into the ethers, just a vague recollection for those with good, long, memories. In fact, about the only remnant of either tower is a boggy area on the east side of Highway 101.

The original water tower served a second purpose: beneath it lay a cranberry bog that furnished fresh cranberries for many Thanksgivings and Christmases at the inn. Today, instead of colorful red berries afloat, the bog is host to a myriad of melodic frogs.

Apparently, the second water tower was considered a work of art, and Marian had plans to turn it into a museum. She had also planned to move the grocery store across the street near the tower, (where the Ultiken place had been), and turn the present-day store into a gift shop.

This is the second water tower that Marian wanted to turn into a museum.

Well, sometimes in life, the best laid plans of man and concessionaire go awry. After the take-over by the park service in 1978, the water tower went the way of the outgoing tide, and the grocery store remains in its original place.

Another of Marian's recollections concerned some of the early park service people who passed her way. Besides Preston Macy and Fred Overly, there was Ike Koontz, the first Kalaloch "ranger." Following Ike was Francis Crouch, and then a gentleman who would later play a large part in Marian Becker's life—Floyd Dickinson.
Floyd, a soft-spoken, fun loving man, was also the one responsible for carving the large log resting in front of Kalaloch's store that reads "Kalaloch Beach Ocean Village."

Floyd made the sign for the Beckers, and it rests there still today, not much the worse for the wear.

The name on the log was eventually changed.

*The original sign for Becker's
Ocean Resort was hand-crafted by Floyd Dickinson.*

The original dining room in the new Inn.

One fact the author was unaware of until research was well under way for this book: there was a "dumbwaiter" that ran between the coffee shop on the main level and the bar upstairs. The dumbwaiter was used when the bar was upstairs where the Kalaloch Suite of today is, and in the coffee shop, it opened up next to the old milkshake machine. It saved a lot of ups and downs for all concerned, delivering food to the bar and drinks to the dining room. When the Kalaloch Suite was built, the dumbwaiter was covered over and is another feature of the lodge that will remain out back of the beyond.

Not only did Marian Becker wear a lot of hats in her day-to-day routine, this talented lady also designed the dishes (plates, cups, saucers, etc.) that graced the tables of Becker's for a lot of years.

When all was said and done, fifty-eight years of serving the public came to an end, and most of the dishes were sold, except for the ones Marian has in her personal collection.

Dishes weren't the only things Marian had to keep track of. Menus were another concern. Famed artist, Elton Bennett was a Becker family friend who stayed at the lodge occasionally, and in the early years, his silk screen prints would sell for around $6. The price for an original Bennett is now in the thousands, but for Marian, he designed the cover of the menu.

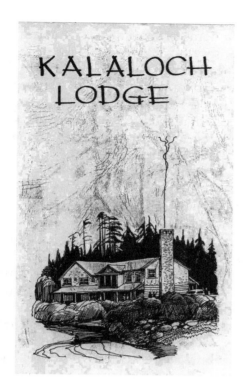

Left: One of the first "menu" covers designed for Marian Becker by famed artist Elton Bennett.

KALALOCH LODGE

SOUPS

BOSTON CLAM CHOWDER .... Bowl ..60		Cup 30
SOUP OF THE DAY .... Bowl ... .30		Cup .... .20
OYSTER MILK STEW			1.00
OYSTER CREAM STEW			1.25

FROM OUR SALAD BAR

SPECIAL KALALOCH CRAB LOUIE with 1.000 Island Dressing ... 2.25
CHEF'S SPECIAL SALAD 1.25
CRAB SALAD BOWL 1.75
FRUIT SALAD BOWL Topped with Sherbet & Whipped Cream . 1.50
PEACH, PEAR or PINEAPPLE with COTTAGE CHEESE 1.25

SANDWICHES

HOT ROAST MEAT SANDWICH 1.25
COLD ROAST MEAT SANDWICH .... .75
KALALOCH CRAB SANDWICH, FRENCH FRIES 1.25
HAMBURGER ..... .60 .... DELUXE ..... .70
CHEESEBURGER .... .75
DENVER SANDWICH, FRENCH FRIES 1.25
OYSTER SANDWICH, FRENCH FRIES 1.25
BACON, LETTUCE and TOMATO .... .80
HOT DOG .... .50
CHEESE SANDWICH .... .50
TOASTED or GRILLED CHEESE SANDWICH ...... .60
BAKED HAM SANDWICH .... .75
FRIED HAM SANDWICH .... .70
FRIED HAM and EGG SANDWICH .... .90
TUNA FISH SANDWICH .... .60
SIDE OF FRENCH FRIES .... .25

FOUNTAIN

MALTED MILK ...... .45
MILK SHAKE ...... .40
FAMOUS HAY'S ICE CREAM . .20
FANCY SUNDAE .... .40
PLAIN SUNDAE .... .30
ROOT BEER FLOAT .. .35

PASTRY

HOMEMADE PIE or CAKE .. .30
WILD BLACKBERRY PIE ... .45
(in season)
WILD HUCKLEBERRY PIE .. .45
(in season)
CREAM PIES .... .45
HOMEMADE BUTTERHORN . .35
HOMEMADE CINNAMON ROLL . .30

BEVERAGES

COFFEE .... .10	TEA .... .15
MILK .... .15	SANKA .... .15
HOT CHOCOLATE .... .20	BUTTERMILK ..... .10

DINNER MENU

APPETIZERS

CRAB COCKTAIL Supreme ... 1.25 Dinner Size .... .60
FRUIT COCKTAIL Dinner Size. .35 TOMATO JUICE ..... .25

ENTREES

SOUP DU JOUR .... DINNER SALAD

SEA FOODS

LOBSTER TAIL ON BED OF LETTUCE, Lemon Butter 4.50
DEEP FRIED CRAB LEGS, Tartar Sauce 3.75
KALALOCH SHORE DINNER, Tartar Sauce 3.50
DEEP FRIED LOUISIANA PRAWNS, Tartar Sauce 3.35
GRILLED RAZOR CLAMS, Cole Slaw 3.25
GRILLED SALMON STEAK, Lemon Butter 3.25
GRILLED HOOD'S CANAL OYSTERS, Lemon Wedge 2.85
DEEP SEA SCALLOPS, Cole Slaw 2.40

STEAKS and CHOPS

NEW YORK CUT SIRLOIN STEAK 5.00
SPENCER STEAK 4.00
TOP SIRLOIN STEAK 4.00
CHOICE DINNER STEAK 3.25
HAMBURGER STEAK 2.50
GRILLED PORK CHOPS 3.00
HOMEMADE BREAD
POTATO .... VEGETABLE
COFFEE .. TEA .. MILK
DINNER DESSERT
SIDE OF FRENCH FRIED ONION RINGS or MUSHROOMS SAUTE .50

CHILD'S PLATE 1.75

CHOICE OF ENTREES:
ROAST OF THE DAY. PORK CHOPS . SALMON . PRAWNS . HAMBURGER STK.
VEGETABLE. POTATO. MILK . DINNER DESSERT

Homemade ITALIAN SPAGHETTI.. TOSSED SALAD GREEN GODDESS DRESSING HOMEMADE BREAD COFFEE..TEA..MILK 1.75	Served ..at.. ANYTIME	HAM & EGGS with HASH BROWNS Homemade TOAST & JAM COFFEE..TEA..MILK 1·50

SPECIAL DIET PLATE 2.00

An early menu shows the fare offered to Kalaloch's visitors.

In the early 1960s, the Beckers began building "a home of their own." According to one of the terms of their twenty-year contract with the park service, a "manager's residence" was to be built, and it MUST be habitable by December 31, 1964.

Bill worked day and night to complete the project, doing most of the building by himself with a bit of help from locals and employees. Working at the lodge all day, Bill then worked late into the nights to complete the house on schedule. A pace that soon took its toll. One snowy December morning, while trying to thaw frozen pipes with a wrench in his hand William Becker had a heart attack and died.

With help from her mother, father, and children, Marian Becker forged on. Then, with help from twenty or so faithful employees, and a brief extension finagled from the park service, the house was complete, including cement sidewalks that the park people felt were so important.

Suddenly, Marian was thrown into a world of men, a lady concessionaire in a previously "good-old-boys' club." She went to the big meetings in places like Yosemite and Williamsburg, Virginia. All along the way she had offers from big corporations to buy her small oceanside business—no dice. She hung onto hers and Bill's dream.

Despite her loss, and the struggles that followed, Marian realized that to remain stagnant at this point would bring failure. So, with determination and sound judgment Seacrest House (the motel unit), as well as Macy and Overly cabins were added.

A few years after Bill's death, Floyd Dickinson, who was the Kalaloch Ranger and a friend of the Beckers for forty years, proposed to Marian. She accepted, and they were married for thirty years, an amazing couple. [11]

Floyd Dickinson

11. *Floyd was a welcome and very helpful addition in my interviews with Marian. Sadly, he passed away earlier this year (1998). Wherever he may be, thank you Floyd.*

In 1977 times really changed, and after more than fifty years of serving the vacationing public and the community, Marian Becker Dickinson left her much loved Kalaloch. For a brief time, Marian's son with Bill Becker, (Skip), ran the resort, but when the contract changed with the park service, fifty-eight years of Becker's Cabin Camp was no more.

After the Beckers were gone, in 1978, Larry and Marge Lesley took over as the new concessionaires for the resort. They were instrumental in building the second row of cabins known as the "logs," and they ran both Kalaloch and Lake Quinault Lodge until 1989.
In 1989 the current concessionaire, ARAMARK, bid on and was awarded the contract.
Recently the log cabins have been re-sided on the outside, and many of the old "view" cabins have been upgraded with new kitchen facilities, new showers, and new roofing has been installed.

Most of the original cabins at Becker's Cabin Camp are mere memories but, as it was in those days long ago, memories are still created on a daily basis at Kalaloch. Marriages are performed, friendships are renewed, and ashes are scattered.

Where the gift shop and front desk are located today, was at one time a lounge for guests. Note the TV set in the corner. There was no TV reception but in Marian's words, "It was an interesting conversation piece."

Razor Clams

Picture left: Cleaning shed used to clean clams, Salmon, and other bounties of the sea.

Yes! Virginia, it realy does snow in Kalaloch.

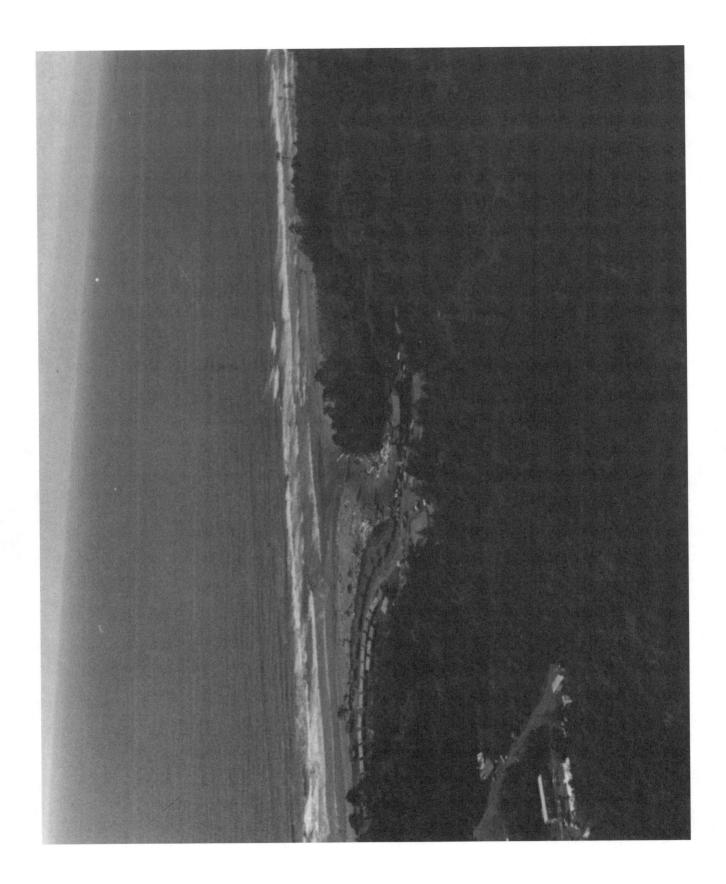

RUBY BEACH

In 1923 life on the peninsula had become so urban that a few enterprising folks decided to set up a gold mining scam. The headlines of the Port Angeles Evening News *on October 4, 1923 screamed:*

WE NEED 3,000
RED BLOODED MEN

To Help Recover One Hundred Million Dollars in Gold, Platinum and Iridium That
Has Been Washed up on the Beach Within a few Days
Journey of Port Angeles

The article went on to say that, untold BILLIONS were to be found in the sands that line almost the whole Pacific Coast. Further claims were made that the "gold" had been valued at from $6 To $600 per ton, and that it would be recovered by "placermining—An Industrial Enterprise—Surer Than Taxes."

And, last but not least:

SHARES NOW SELLING AT $1.00 EACH

A "coupon" at the end of the article was handy so those desiring to participate in this potentially enormous wealth-making enterprise could just clip it out and send it to:

"Ruby Beach Mining Company, Rooms 9 and 10,
Dabney Block, Aberdeen, Washington."

Once again, on November 21, 1923, the Port Angeles Evening News had big headlines:

Work Starts at
RUBY BEACH

This article declared that the president of Ruby Beach Mining Company along with an engineer and crew of workmen were on their way to Ruby Beach to erect camp and, "get things in readiness for the construction of foundations for the recovery plant."

Lo and behold, the next headlines were even better, proclaiming that, "As of November 15th,

SHARES NOW $2 EACH.

"The Board of Directors feel that shares are well worth that figure," and to spice the pot a bit, they further proclaimed:

SHARES WILL BE $3 EACH BY
DECEMBER 23!

What a deal.

As it turned out, the Board of Directors had procured some old gold mining machinery and even brought in a "ball mill" for crushing the ore. They then made arrangements to land a barge south of Abby Island, just off Ruby Beach, where they would "set up" this multi-million dollar operation.

However…Landing the barge wasn't the only arrangement they made. They also arranged a small "wreck" for the barge and for their state-of-the-art equipment. Alas, the venture never got off the ground, or beach, as it were.

Prosecution did follow, but not in Jefferson County. Some of the wealthier, big-time investors from the East, whose sense of adventure and dreams of fabulous wealth from a gold mine on the shores of the Pacific were dashed by the scam, and this caused them to settle the score.

Kalaloch wasn't the only resort on the Coast. By 1940 there were five or six different operations along the ocean strip between the Quillayute River and Kalaloch. Besides Becker's Cabin Camp, there was Ashenbrenner's Pioneer Camp (now South Beach and considered to be part of Kalaloch), La Push Ocean Resort, the Harvey Smith Ranch at La Push, and at Mora there was a resort run by Rozella Andrews. But the most notable "camp" along the beach stretch was at Ruby Beach. Today Ruby Beach is known for its sea-stacks and rugged coastline, but there's more to the story.

Around 1932, John and Elizabeth (Bettine) Fletcher bought forty acres of land. The acreage included Cedar Creek, and there was a natural spring in the northeast corner of the land. A water line led from the spring to a water tank to supply their growing "autocamp" which they'd named Ruby Beach Cabin Camp.

Ruby Beach Cabin Camp.

Besides the lodge, there was a store-building plus fifteen cabins, and by the time Highway 101 opened, there was a service station, dinning room, and light plant.

The store, a two-story structure, had three or four bedrooms upstairs, and there was a small dining room on the main floor. The entire dining room was paneled with hand-hewn cedar shakes, an accomplishment that gave the Fletcher's a great deal of pride. One of the upstairs rooms was extra large and served as a dormitory for some of the employees. The fifteen cabins were arranged with several top-side (near the road), while others were spaced along the trail down towards the beach.

One of the most unique and sought-after cabins offered to fun seekers was cabin eight. Cabin eight was small and cozy, and every June or so, the cabin was set on drift-logs and moved out into the ocean to rock-a-bye its tenants with the ebb and flow of the tides. In September, when the tides became stronger, the cabin was removed from its perch on the logs and placed far enough back towards the bank to avoid damage from winter storms.

John and Bettine had no children of their own, but they did have a large extended family. From an interview with Elizabeth (Missy) Fletcher Barlow, their niece, we get a glimpse of what life was like in those early days at both Ruby Beach, and living life along the Hoh River.

Missy's father, Fred A. Fletcher, moved onto and proved up on a 160 acres on the north side of the Hoh when he was twenty-one. The homestead had been previously claimed, but the claimer had seen bigger fortunes awaiting him in the Alaska Gold Rush and left for more profitable ventures. Her grandfather had a 160 acre homestead just across the river on the south shore with timber rights, and most of this land is still in the family.

The first time Missy remembers going to Ruby Beach was with her Dad when she was six years old. Her Dad was a packer with horses, and he ran supplies in from "the outside world." With a growing business, many supplies brought into Ruby Beach came by wagon after first being brought overland, then John Fletcher freighted them across the Hoh on a little freight boat he owned.

Until 1931 when Highway 101 was finished, families who lived "out" on the west end and had children of high school age had to send the kids by bus into Forks where they were boarded during the school week. From where the road ended, the kids who lived across the river on the south bank had to first be canoed over to the other shore, and then bussed into town. For the younger school age children there was a school nearby, built on land John Fletcher had donated for that purpose. In 1946 the grade school was shut down under the pretext that the "water system" wasn't good enough, but by then Highway 101 was completed and all the kids were bussed to Forks for learnin'.

Missy moved to Ruby Beach when she was thirteen, and Aunt Bettine took her under her wing. In her words, she was, "a backwoods kid," and Aunt Bettine and Uncle John caught her and put shoes on her and gave her a little bringing up. She was one of the "employees" who lived in the dormitory-style room at the lodge, and for her efforts she earned fifty cents a day. Later that was raised to a whole dollar!

Aunt Bettine was a Home-Ec graduate and an excellent cook. What cooking Missy learned to do, she learned from her aunt. Bettine had an old Lange stove about six feet long with a big oven. Missy learned to bake from her aunt who made about thirty-six loaves of bread a day. The loaves were baked in big old logging company bread pans that held three or four loaves in a row, each row two loaves deep. (If you've never cooked or baked on a wood-burning stove, then you'll have to trust me—it's an art form.

Baking wasn't the only job that employees were called upon to perform. They also waited tables, washed dishes, and carried water. Missy and one of her friends had a private joke that if Aunt Bet had to clean up after herself when cooking, she could have it done in short order. But, if the girls had to clean up after her, and Bet had six frying pans, all six of 'em were used. Even working at top speed, the girls were hard pressed to keep up with her.

Aunt Bettine was a doer while Uncle John was a PR man. John loved to talk to people and he was invaluable as a connection with the public, but occasionally, someone had to "round him up" because there were chores that needed doing, and he was hung-up chatting with guests.

All too soon, the Fletchers, and all of the would-be cabin camp entrepreneurs perched along the Kalaloch to Ruby Beach stretch learned that alas, some dreams die.

In 1940, President Roosevelt, at the urging of his advisors declared that a wide corridor of land from Shi Shi Beach to just north of the Queets River become a part of the recently named Olympic National Park.[12] The actions of Roosevelt were consummated by President Harry Truman in 1953, and those settlers who'd built their dreams along the Washington Coast "strip" were forced to relinquish their land.

At that time, the only way any land for a park could legally be acquired was by gift or purchase. So, the government went to court and swore they needed all this land for a PWA (Public Works Association) project. The debate continues still today as to whether or not they ever had any intentions of implementing the project. Prior to final acquisition, emissaries (rather nefarious emissaries) were sent around the area to let on that they were going to build a mill near the mouth of the Queets River and so forth.

These emissaries managed to find the most disillusioned settlers and told them, "If you will sell me your property, then we'll build this mill, and it will be good for the whole area." With no "real" mill in the planning, all they were trying to do was establish the lowest possible price for the property along the strip.

After the land was condemned and taken over by the government, the Fletchers were given the opportunity to stay on and "run" the operation at Ruby Beach for a few years, with only a "yearly" lease and no security at all. To add insult to injury, the restrictions the government placed on all those they'd made the same offer to were so restrictive that it would have been impossible to continue in business for long. Basically, those accepting the government's offer would not be allowed to change, modify, or alter the property in ANY WAY without prior approval. Building repairs would be subject to the discretion of the park service, new buildings would have to be pre-approved, and no trees or land could be cleared without prior approval.

When the Fletchers refused this generous offer, they were told the princely sum they would receive for their life's work—forty acres, plus the fifteen cabins, store, gas station etc.— would be $8,000.00. No, the decimal is not in the wrong place.

After a court battle to increase that sum, the Fletchers were told by their attorney, quite simply, "If you appeal, they're going to continue this and keep continuing it until you run out of money and you just can't go on." They were already out of money.

To add more insult to the family, in the original "strip plans," the Fletcher Family Homestead along the Hoh (Fred and Lena Fletcher's place) was going to be included in the acquisition. It had been run through the condemnation process but Lena Huelsdonk Fletcher (Missy's Mother) mounted a voluminous letter writing campaign to every politician of the time, trying to save her family's homestead. In the end, the homestead was not taken, and Lena Fletcher was

12. *This corridor was originally set to contain much more land than it has today..*

told privately that, "We're not gonna take your property. We're not gonna take it, but you're going to wish we had because you're gonna be stuck with the court costs." And they were.[13]

When World War II interrupted the lives of many Americans, the Fletchers were no exception. After the park service took control of Ruby Beach, the Fletchers were given a deadline by which they had to move. With the onset of the war the deadline was abruptly cut short, and they were forced to leave their home when the Armed Forces took over their living quarters. Mrs. Barlow remembers having every nook and cranny of their homestead on the Hoh filled with her Aunt and Uncle's belongings.

In the end, all privately owned resorts, including Beckers were purchased by the park service in the take-over of the strip. With the exception of Kalaloch, all other facilities were eliminated, but the saddest, most bitter memory for Missy Barlow was the fact that rather than remove all the facilities and place them elsewhere, the park service chose to burn them down, "hand-hewn" cedar shakes and all.

NOTE: Elizabeth (Missy) Barlow lives with her husband Charles, on the Fletcher Family homestead. Both have degrees in Botany. Missy has a quick wit and a keen mind. She is also an exceptionally fine artist and sells her work through the "Olympic West Arttrek" Association.

Smelt dippers at Ruby Beach try their hand at capturing the small silvery fish

13.   *Fifteen years after the Fletcher's were forced to pay the court costs, Washington's Senator Henry Jackson put a bill through Congress to reimburse them. In the end they received around $22,000 which still isn't a great deal of money by today's standards, and nothing can repay the loss of dignity they suffered.*

Ruby Beach Ocean Resort. This photo is of the main lodge.

KALALOCH TODAY

The most often asked question at Kalaloch is, "How do you pronounce the name?" The question is usually followed by an attempt on the asker's part to take a stab at it: "Cal-a-looch? Ka-la-lock? Cal-a-lock?" All of which are good, sound, honest tries. They're all wrong, but that's okay. It's rare that anyone comes close. The correct pronunciation, as we know it today, is "Clay-lock." (In my interview with Marian Becker Dickinson, she said in the early days the name was pronounced "Kalay-ka-lo.")

The second most asked question is, "What does Kalaloch mean?" Well, that's a little tougher to answer. The two most popular versions of the meaning today seem to be, "Land of Many Clams" or "Safe Landing." At this point in time, the true meaning is anyone's guess, and those who knew the real meaning are now paddling dugouts in the sky, so we'll all have to settle for a vague interpretation.

"Where are you?" is another question we hear. If you look at a map, you'll discover that Kalaloch is not that easy to find. The fact that Kalaloch really isn't a "city," all the little dots, stars, and circles those map folks apply to most places, aren't going to help much.

For those of you who are directionally challenged, all you have to do is find Seattle. (Hint: Look for a lot of water; it's usually colored blue). Once you have Seattle in your sights, take a string, place one end on Seattle proper, and head west (or left) towards the Pacific Ocean. (If you can't find the Pacific Ocean, you need a lot more directional help than we can give you here.) When your left hand string reaches the Pacific, it will most likely rest on a small town named Queets. Look a short five miles north (up). We're usually shown as the Kalaloch Rocks, and there we are.

Now that you've found Kalaloch on the map, the next step is to find Highway 101.

Highway 101 semi-circles the Olympic Peninsula, and whether you choose to go north or south, Kalaloch is roughly one hundred and eighty miles away from Seattle—unless you're a crow. In that case you'd be able to fly along the string line for roughly ninety miles and not have to deal with ferries, stop signs, and road construction.

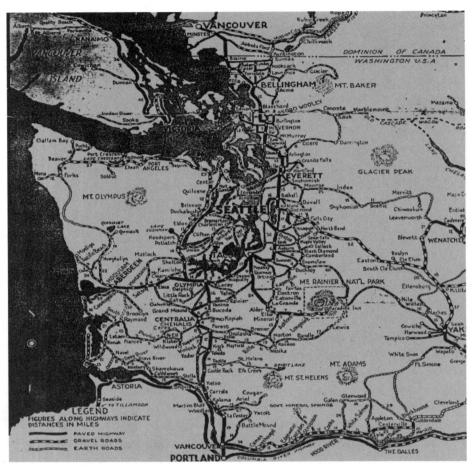

This old map shows a temporary road from Forks to just north of Lake Quinault. The dotted lines are "gravel" roads and the solid lines show paved higways.

What is a Kalaloch? This is the toughest question to answer because Kalaloch is many things to many people. To the National Park Service, Kalaloch is encompassed in the tail-end of a narrow strip of land, about a mile wide at the widest that runs north from three miles above the Queets River drainage for seventy miles to Shi Shi Beach at the edge of the Makah Indian Reservation. This narrow strip of land was acquired by the park service in 1940 under the guidance of President Franklin D. Roosevelt. The "strip" became part of Olympic National Park when the deal was consummated and signed into law when President Harry S. Truman signed his final official proclamation in 1953. The strip encompasses the Hoh, Quileute, and Ozette Indian Reservations and is host to numerous creeks, streams, and rivers that wend their way to the Pacific Ocean.

In 1994 an offshore stretch of the Pacific Ocean was made into a marine sanctuary. Known as the Olympic Coast National Marine Sanctuary, the area runs south from Cape Flattery to Copalis Rock and reaches thirty to forty miles offshore. This sanctuary is as unique as the rest of Olympic National Park and is now protected from all offshore oil and gas drilling. Ships carrying hazardous cargoes are asked to avoid these sensitive areas. The designation has helped many previously threatened ocean communities to begin rebuilding.

To the Indian tribes who lived along the coast, and took an abundance of sustenance from the sea, this strip of land was life. Their children were born here and died here. They loved, laughed, and cried here. War canoes were launched from these shores to do battle with neighboring tribes as well as battle with the elements. These canoes, made out of a single cedar tree, were large enough to hold many warriors and were sent into the wild surf to hunt for whales that were twice the size of the dugouts. Kalaloch is one of the few places along the Washington Coast where the natives could land a canoe safely.

To those who first settled along the rivers and smaller streams like Kalaloch Creek that flowed into the mighty Pacific Ocean, the coastal strip of land was a new beginning. The land would test their metal and force them to forge a hard new life out of a wilderness.

Life in this rain forest was never easy. Whether sinner or saint, Indian or white man, one lived by one's wits or moved on.

When the government came in and the tribes found themselves relegated to reservations, there were some very unhappy natives around. And, as with the Indians, when the government came in and preempted the settlers' land for a national park—well, let's just say that even after many decades, there are still some folks around with a bad taste in their mouths.

All that is in the past, a done deal, and those who now visit Kalaloch quickly find it is Paradise, Nirvana, and Shangri-La all rolled into one. The famous Kalaloch Rocks, the awesome piles of bleached, water-logged driftwood, and the unbeatable sunsets continue to play host to weddings, family reunions, anniversaries, births, funerals, and to people who are just "getting away from it all." All manner of rites are celebrated at Kalaloch every year, and the number of shutters that click just to ensure a lasting memory seem like enough to support the film industry on an annual basis.

An example of the beauties of Kalaloch and the power of the ocean can be seen from the bluff in front of the lodge. If you stand on the bluff and look north, you'll see a huge upright tree trunk down in the creek. Anytime you doubt the power of the ocean tides, think about this trunk. The origins of this behemoth are uncertain, but in current form it began its beach walk thirty years ago down by South Beach—three miles away. Every year, with the fierce Pacific storms of winter, this tree has drifted, (always in an upright position) to its present location. In the summer of 1996 the stump was about even with the last set of cabins, a thousand yards south of the Kalaloch Beach Trail. In one fierce, three-day storm, we watched it hurtle up the creek, turn the corner, and come to rest some 500 yards or better up stream.

Beach Logs along Kalaloch Beacch.
Photos courtesy of James Ball.

Kalaloch encompasses a Park information/Ranger Station, the Kalaloch Lodge, and Kalaloch Campground, all situated along a one mile stretch of Highway 101.

On the north side of Kalaloch Lodge is the campground with 175 RV spaces and tent sites. None of the sites have power hookups. There is an RV dump station, and twenty-one feet is about the maximum length for RV's. Although, there are a few exceptions. The campground is open year-round, serviced by the park service, and run on a first-come-first-served basis: no reservations. Of the 175 campsites, only thirty or so are situated along a steep bluff overlooking the ocean. Needless to say, these are the most sought after spaces. The maximum length of stay is fourteen days, and the fee is $12 per unit per day, $6 per day with a Golden Age passport. A maximum of eight people per site is enforced, as is one vehicle per space. (There's an overflow parking/ picnic area.)

If the campground is full, try South Beach, about three and a half miles south of the main site. The fee is $8, but there is no potable water. Both sites are strictly a first-come-first-served arrangement. Tenters as well as RV's use South Beach, but RVer's should be aware that the road into the area is steep and rough.

Camping on the beach is prohibited and wouldn't be a real bright idea. We get fierce high tides, and unless you're into waking up to waves and logs crashing around you, over you, under you, etc., camp ONLY in designated campsites.

During the summer months, an amphitheater located near the "A" loop in the main campground is host to a variety of ranger talks in the evenings. These informative orations will fill you in on everything from Sitka Spruce to the Roosevelt Elk. On Sunday's at 7:30 p.m., there is a Christian Ministry church service in the amphitheater.

To the south of Kalaloch Lodge (about a quarter of a mile on the opposite side of the highway) is the ranger station/information center. The information center is open daily 8 a.m. to 4:30 p.m. from mid-May until after Labor Day. The friendly folks there are an excellent source for facts about Olympic National Park and Kalaloch.

Also during the summer months, in conjunction with Kalaloch Lodge, there are daily ranger-guided tours of beaches, tide pools, trails, and rain forests. Information on tours can be obtained at the lodge front desk and the ranger station. Or, if you're the do-it-yourself type, there are miles and miles of sandy beaches to explore, as well as inland hiking trails.

A few things you should keep in mind: For those of you who can't bear to leave Fido at home remember, you're in a National Park and your best friend MUST BE ON A LEASH AT ALL TIMES, even on the beach. There's a $50 fine every time you're caught "leashless." And, by the way, bring a "pooper-scooper," and use it.

A FEW MORE QUESTIONS ANSWERED
- Can we build a fire on the beach?
  Yes, BUT it must be more than ten feet away from the nearest beach log, and must not be more than three feet in diameter. Driftwood and dead and down wood may be used—DO NOT CUT LIVE VEGETATION or use chainsaws.[14]
- Can we camp on the beach?
  Camping is permitted on the Olympic Coast EXCEPT: between Ellen Creek and Rialto Beach and on ALL beaches south of the Hoh River, including Kalaloch Beaches.

Everyone at Kalaloch wants you to enjoy your time with us. The Park Rangers, the hosts at the campgrounds, and we of Kalaloch Lodge will do our best to make your visit enjoyable.

As the slogan goes: "Getting here is easy. It's the leaving that is hard."

14   If there has been a long dry spell the park service will post notices that beach fires are banned. Please adhere to these notices.

Scenes of Kalaloch.

WHAT DO WE DO WHEN WE GET THERE?

So, you're planning the big trip. You're going to do a whirlwind tour of Olympic National Park. Your plane lands in Seattle, and you have a glorious three days to see everything. GOOD LUCK!

For starters, Olympic isn't a Yellowstone or a Yosemite where you can drive to a viewpoint, take a few devastatingly brilliant pictures, and head for the next scenic vista. There are no roads that run through the center of the park, although there have been proposals for such in the past. The Olympic Mountains have pretty well put the kibosh on the road program, so if crossing the interior of the park is your desire, you'd best purchase a sturdy pair of hiking boots and a backpack, because there are some six-hundred miles of hiking trails that crisscross the mountains.

If automobile travel is your choice of transportation, you'll soon discover the roads that do pierce the interior of the park vary in length and are "dead ends. This means the road you enter the park on is the same road you exit on. Kalaloch is the exception.

If you are visiting, or planning to visit Kalaloch for the first time, there are a few things you should be aware of: If you're expecting a Disneyland or amusement park atmosphere you're going to be very disappointed. We get no cell-phone reception for five miles either side of the Lodge, and there are only two TVs—both hooked up to Primestar cable. One TV is in the Kalaloch Suite, the other is in the Becker Suite. During the summer, both suites are view rooms in the main lodge; during the winter the Becker Suite is converted to a library, where all guests are welcome to relax and enjoy the fireplace, TV (with VCR) and a panoramic view of the ocean. None of our rooms have a telephone, but there are five pay phones available on the premises.

All but six of our cabins have kitchens, some with ovens some without. If you're planning on cooking up a storm while you're here best be prepared to bring all of your own pots, pans, dishes, utensils, dish soap, etc. None are provided.

Speaking of "storms," if you're planning on a winter visit, be prepared. We get fierce Pacific storms, and extremely high winds. Our electric power source is based in Aberdeen—seventy-five miles south. That's a long distance filled with a whole bunch of trees; trees that just love to bounce off of power lines. The problem is they only bounce once—if at all, and the lines come tumbling down. The lodge does have an adequate number of oil-burning candles to distribute to guests but the light they give off is minimal. It would be a good idea to throw in a florescent lantern or a couple of high power flashlights—just in case.[15] Most of the cabins have wood-burning stoves, and those cabins that don't, have propane stoves that can be used as a heat source.

On those cold winter nights when cooking by candle light doesn't sound all that great, our lodge kitchen is fueled by propane so meals can still be served in the lodge.

If you've never seen a winter storm over the ocean it is truly a thing of beauty. A storm would also answer any questions you may have as to, "where did all those big logs come from?" There are a number of people who watch the weather forecasts and book a cabin if a storm is predicted. Few are disappointed. But if winter travel isn't your bag, come on down in the summer. We have sunsets to die for and who wouldn't love to take a moonlit walk on a sandy beach with pale phosphorescent moonbows dancing off the surf.

The main lodge has an excellent restaurant that serves breakfast, lunch, and dinner; a coffee shop/cocktail lounge, a gift shop; and the "original" Kalaloch Store, though slightly modified, is still selling gas and groceries.

We don't have a Marian or a Barney, but we do have indoor plumbing, and if you're a nostalgia buff longing for the good-old-days, we can probably bribe one of our friendly staff to ask you, "Now what the hell do you want?"

EXPLORING THE COAST

On your way to Kalaloch you most likely noticed a number of beach trail signs. Beach trails one and two are south of the lodge, and to the north are trails three, four, six, and Ruby Beach. Wondering what happened to trails five, seven, and eight? Well, they were in existence at one time, but the ocean tends to reclaim its own. However, if you look close….[16] Of the remaining trails, Beach Trail Four, and Ruby Beach are the most popular, and if your time with us is short, these are the two you should put on your list as "Must Sees."

Beach Four is host to a myriad of tidal pools, seen best at LOW tide. Actually, they can only be seen at low tide. What's a tidal pool? A tidal pool is a mini-community of sea-life. Mussels are one of the most prominent species in these "pools," and they provide an environment that affects 300 other species from ochre sea stars (or starfish) that dine on mussels to ribbon worms that hide among the shells from predators to barnacles that use their shells anchoring them to anything that holds still long enough. You'll also see whelks, sea anemones, limpets, and sea urchins.

Besides the intertidal life, if you're really lucky, you may spot a river otter, harbor seal, or sea lion on the beach[17] or in the water. Out to sea, in the fall and spring of the year, watch the

---

15. *Propane lanterns aren't that safe in an enclosed area and it's preferred they not be used.*
16. *You may also be wondering why numbers instead of names for the beaches. The only explanation the author could come up with is: When the first settlers came through, the least of their worries was naming places?*
17. *Seal mothers often push their pups ashore to protect them while Mom feeds in the ocean. Please DON'T try to play humanitarian of the year and "save" the pup; it doesn't need your help, and in most cases you'll cause more harm than imaginable - plus they bite.*

far horizon for whales. Gray whales usually pass closer to shore than sperm whales, but both pass by on their bi-annual migrations.

Whale watching tips: Early morning hours, before winds cause whitecaps are usually more favorable, or evenings are good as back-lighting from the setting sun can be helpful. Over cast days are best because there's less glare. Scan the horizon and look for "blows," water blown into the air up to 12 feet when the whale exhales. Once you've seen a blow, concentrate on the same area. Where you see one, you should see others either from the same whale or others in the same pod.

While you're on the beach if you watch the sky over head, you'll also see a large variety of bird life, everything from a bald eagle to a California gull. There are cormorants (the gangly looking birds with wings stretched out to dry their feathers), tufted puffins, terns, common crows, and ravens.

While you're watching the heavens, be sure you watch your step, especially in the inter-tidal area. It's kind of like the old song says, "The foot bone's connected to the ankle bone, the ankle bone's connected to the leg bone," and so on. All intertidal life is in some manner con-nected to its neighbor. These living organisms must withstand drying sun and pounding surf according to tidal actions, and they are ALL very easily damaged by a careless footstep whether that misplaced foot has the weight of mom or dad, child or Rover. Some sea urchins and mussels can live for 50 years while sea anemones may reach the ripe old age of 1,000 years. So, before you poke that stick in that funny looking green thing to see it curl up, think about the amount of damage you'd suffer if you were a thousand years old and someone stuck a stick in your "eye." Just DON'T do it!

Once you pry yourself away from beach four or the tide comes in, whichever is first, head on up the highway to Ruby Beach. Ruby Beach is so named because of the garnet colored rocks found there — or so the story goes — and is known for its sea stacks.

A sea stack is a mound of rock that many years ago was the headland, and a headland is that piece of ground you're standing on above the beach while looking at a sea stack. The softer soil around this mound of rocks was washed away by the ocean tides, leaving the harder sub-stances intact. As time and tide ebb and flow, eventually the pounding surf will reduce even the sea stacks to beach pebbles and the headland to sea stacks.

Ruby Beach is also known for smelt dipping. Smelt are small silvery fish that inhabit both the ocean and freshwater streams. At certain times of the year, according to their eons-old biological clocks, smelt thrash ashore to continue their species by laying offspring in gravel beds; Ruby Beach is perfect. When the smelt are "running," as it's called, folks get out there with huge, fine-meshed nets and scoop the fish from the surf. Then they cook and eat them.

The small stream running into the surf here is Cedar Creek. If you can, imagine the cabin Missy Barlow described floating on the ocean swells. Then, pull up a drift log, have a seat, and relax into oblivion. As Missy Barlow said, "There's a lot of beauty along the Washington Coast, but nothing can match Ruby Beach for the scenery."

If solitude is your "bag" try beach six. It's a bit of a hike to get down to or up from but well worth the effort. Your only concern here should be high tide, so keep one eye open while you snooze on the sands. Beach six is also a good place to watch for whales because sometimes they swim by between the headland and Destruction Island rather than farther out to sea.

Beach one, from the car-park to the beach goes through a spruce forest. The trunks of many of the trees have large burls, and many have a variety of polypores, which are members of the mushroom family, clinging to their bark.

With all the beaches in the area, caution and alertness should go hand-in-hand. Swimming is discouraged because of the strong undertow and rip tides not to mention huge logs that weigh thousands of pounds yet are tossed around in the surf like match sticks. If one of those lands on you, you'll earn your angel wings early.

HUNTERS AND GATHERERS

Early man lived in what is known as a "hunter gatherer" society. They hunted for wild game and gathered wild seeds for survival. When you think about it, modern man isn't that much different, as far as the hunt and gather bit go. We're still doing it; only now, some of the things we hunt and gather aren't for our survival, and we can cause a lot of damage.

Think about it. Every time we go to the beach, whether we're five or fifty-five years old, we all tend to hunt and gather: rocks, driftwood, sand. If we'd all just stick to pebbles and bits of wood, things would be a whole bunch better. However, the gathering of sea "life" is a whole different story. Sea stars, tube worms, and sand dollars are NOT fair game, nor are seal pups, injured birds, or river otters.

It doesn't take much to upset the balance of nature. One tube worm plucked from a colony can, and often does destroy the rest. Sand dollars that look like they're covered in fuzzy wiggly things ARE ALIVE. Injured birds can impart a life-threatening disease to those who decide to "nurse" them.

So, hunt and gather if you must: hunt for those agates, gather that driftwood, but PLEASE!!! leave the sea-life alone!

Moss Laden Trees in the Hoh Rain Forest.

OTHER SITES ALONG THE COAST

The most intriguing sight along this stretch of Highway 101 is Destruction Island. According to those who research these kinds of things, geologists and such, Destruction Island wasn't always an island—maybe. There is a chance that at one time it was part of the mainland, and due to the nature of its rock structure, it has remained intact while the softer, more easily eroded ground around it has been swept away. Today it stands some three miles off the mainland, and inch by inch, year by year, the distance increases.

An arial shot of Destruction Island shows the rugged coastline.

The Destruction Island Light House.

The island's surface measures about eight and a half football fields long and is around three hundred yards wide at its widest. The topside of Destruction is ninety feet from its base—give or take where you want to place the base.

The native name for the island was "ta tchist qu" and, it was also called "Hoh to la bish." When white people arrived, the island was given several names over the years. It was shown on very early nautical maps as "Green Island," supposedly named for the abundance of green vegetation thereon. Heceta and Quadra, (possible others) called it "Isla de Dolores" or land of Sorrows. Another sea captain who lost his ship near the mouth of Hoh River christened the river "Destruction River," and the name seems to have carried over to the land.

Is-

the

is-

The origianl Destruction Island sign graced Highway 101 for a long time.

When the Hoh Tribe won a hard fought struggle for sovereignty over their lands, the river's name was changed to "Hoh," but the island has remained Destruction. It's also almost certain that due to the surrounding reef-like rocks skirting much of the island, which are well-concealed at high tide, fishermen who have plied these waters over the years have called the island names that won't be recited here.

Should you have a burning desire to tour the island, you may just have to be satisfied with a powerful pair of binoculars and a 400mm camera lens. Since its inclusion in the Marine Sanctuary, it's off-limits, and landing is prohibited except by special permit.

Ownership of the island is debatable. The Hoh Tribe claims it as part of their heritage from as far back as their original ancestors who walked and sailed these shores some ten to twelve-thousand years ago. The U.S. government claimed it, placed a lighthouse atop it in 1885, and when the coastal Marine Sanctuary came into being, the island was placed under its protection. While the debate of ownership goes on, King Neptune will ultimately have the last word.

The lightkeepers quarters on Destruction Island.

View from the lighthouse tower looking northeast.

If more sights along the Washington Coast are your priority, be forewarned, it's not going to be a cake-walk. Other than Rialto Beach and La Push, which can be driven to, the other beaches are gained only by foot; horses and bikes are NOT allowed.

To explore the beaches between Kalaloch and Shi Shi first get a tide chart and a good map. Then check conditions with the local ranger and ask about areas in which to exercise extreme caution. Hiking a deserted beach isn't nearly as much fun when you discover the tide has crept up on you, and the only option you have of saving yourself is clinging to a slippery tree stump hanging out of a cliff (if there is one) as the waves wash over you. IT HAPPENS EVERY YEAR! Please don't let it happen to you.

A sturdy pair of hiking boots is a pretty good idea too. Tie the laces together and throw them over your shoulder if you can't stand to be at the beach with shoes on. Sometimes, getting from a headland to the beach is not barefoot friendly.

If you're a hiker, look at the Olympic "Official Map and Guide." You'll find a couple of "Memorial" sites listed that should pique your interest, for example, the Norwegian Memorial and the Chilean Memorial. The Chilean Memorial is located four and half miles north of Rialto Beach at Cape Johnson. Marked by a concrete monument are the graves of a woman and five men who died October 3rd, 1891, when the Chilean ship, Lenore, wrecked in gale-force winds.

Remarkably, not quite thirty years later on November 11th, 1920 another Chilean ship, the W. J. Pirrie, was driven shoreward by ninety mile per hour winds where it was crushed on the offshore rocks. Already a distressed ship, the Pirrie was in tow by the Santa Rita, a lumber barge. The Santa Rita's captain realized his vessel was also in serious danger, so he cut the tow line as the two ships foundered about 800 yards off shore. Because of the two wrecks, this area of beach is sometimes referred to as the "Beach of the Dead."

The Norwegian Memorial is located about two miles from the southern end of Lake Ozette. It's a small rock monument placed on the site where the Prince Arthur, a ship piloted by Captain Hans Markusson, smashed upon the rocks on January 2, 1903.

A storm was raging and the captain thought he'd seen a light off the starboard side. Assuming he was at Cape Flattery and the light he'd seen was the Tatoosh Island lighthouse that marks the mouth of the Strait of Juan de Fuca, he turned his ship to the right. It was his last turn. The ship broke in two in the heavy seas and eighteen men, including the captain died.

MOUTH OF THE HOH RIVER

If you've always wanted to see where the Hoh River penetrates the Pacific, you can get there by car—almost.

Around eighteen miles north of Kalaloch (before you reach the Hoh Rain Forest turnoff) is Oil City Road. Oil City Road is not for the faint of heart, nor the bald of tire. The road is paved in short stretches until you're about five miles in, then a branch-road forks to the left at Cotton-wood Campground. Shortly thereafter, a sign announcing "Primitive Road" lets you know the remainder of your trip will be on a washboard-bedeviled, pothole-infested, gravel-strewn ribbon of highway. And did I mention the dust?

"Oil City Road, you say. Is there an Oil City?" Well, there was of a sorts. In 1931, oil seepage near Hoh Head led some folks to believe "black gold" was there for the taking. The construction company that built Oil City Road called the small town that sprang up near the seepage Oil City.

Oil well rigging was brought in along with lumber to construct a derrick, and even an oil well cover or two was optimistically included so they wouldn't lose their bonanza. And they built, and they sweated, and they drilled—and they went bust. No oil.

Oil City Road remains, running parallel to the Hoh River, and up until about seventeen years ago, you could drive all the way to the Pacific Ocean. Then, one stormy fateful day, the Hoh River took back a piece of real estate. The final bridge to the ocean washed out and was last seen headed for Tokyo. You can still get to the ocean; it's just going to have to be afoot.[18]

18.   *A word of caution here. Hoh Head is one of those nasty places the park service cautions you about. It is NOT passable by beach.*

RIALTO BEACH

Rialto Beach is another of the few beaches to which you can drive. Drive north through the town of Forks and turn left (west) on State Road 110. Three miles from where you started, the road forks. If you turn left, you'll be on the La Push Road. If you go right, you'll be on the Quillayute Road. The Quillayute Road will connect you to the Mora road and take you straight to Rialto Beach. The La Push Road will also connect you to the Mora Road, if you take a right at the second fork, or it will take you to La Push. (It's easier than it sounds, and if all else fails, get a map.) Rialto is located on the north side of the Quillayute[19] River, and can be a starting point for a hike to the Chilean Memorial. Or, just curl up on one of the huge drift logs and relax.

At one time there was a long breakwater constructed of enormous boulders to keep the exceptionally rough surf from inundating the town of La Push, which is on the south bank of the Quillyute River. There was also a large, "double" parking lot adjacent to the beach on the north side and more driftwood than most beaches see in an eon. In February or March of 1996, the power of the Pacific let itself be known. Almost the entire breakwater, as well as half of the double parking lot succumbed to a horrific storm. Chunks of blacktop rest on the few drift logs that weren't carried out to sea or buried under tons of sand. Even so, Rialto Beach is still a remarkable place. Watch for seals and eagles—and watch the tide.

From the La Push side of the Quillayute, you can hike .6 miles to Second Beach. The beach is two miles long with sea stacks and tidal pools. A mile from Second Beach is Third Beach.

LAKE OZETTE

The first white settlers in the Lake Ozette area were of Scandinavian descent. At one time, there were around five hundred inhabitants, and in a few places there is still evidence of their lives. When the area was included in the strip acquisition, the park service removed most of the structures, and those that were left have long since begun to deteriorate.

To get to Lake Ozette, take Highways 113 and 112 to Clallam Bay. Turn off at the Hoko-Ozette Road and travel twenty-one miles to the ranger station. The area encompasses fifty-seven miles of coastal wilderness. A three-mile planked trail will lead you to Sand Point on the ocean. If you wish, hike north along the beach where you'll find Indian petroglyphs at Wedding Rocks. From Sand Point, it's three miles to Cape Alava, where the Ozette archeological dig took place. The site is closed but marked with a small sign. From Cape Alava, a 3.1 mile hike, also on cedar planks, will take you back to the ranger station. Be sure to take lots of film; seals, deer, eagles, osprey, otters and whales may be seen.

If you own a powerboat, canoe, or kayak, Lake Ozette is great for boating. There are a couple of campsites (one is boat-in only), and as with most lakes, canoeists should beware of occasional high afternoon winds.

If you're curious about the almost obsidian color of the lake's water, be curious no more; it's caused by tannin. Tannin is present in many trees and plant life and leeches into the water, imparting a deep reddish color. The volume of the tannin makes the water appear black.

The Lake Ozette ocean-side area allows camping on the beach only in designated areas.

---

19. *The spelling of the Quillayute River is different than the spelling of the Quillaute Tribe or Quileute Reservation. All spellings refer to the same Native Americans.*

Because of budget restriction, there are limited services available at Lake Ozette. For instance, there is no trash service, and so you must pack out all your own trash—please.

Another view of Destruction Island and a slightly modified sign from the original.

OF WEATHER AND CRITTERS AND FIRS

WEATHER

To repeat an old saying, "Everybody complains about the weather, but nobody does anything about it."[20]

At Kalaloch, the weather has a mind and temper of its own. When one lives between two rain forests, one had better expect some rain. Or, to put it another way, the only way you know it's spring at Kalaloch is, the rain is warmer. August and September seem to be the best months with the least amount of rain that is, but don't bet on it. When you choose to visit an area where the annual average rainfall is 144 inches a year, 200 plus on occasion, plan on getting wet.

Does it snow at Kalaloch? Yes it does, occasionally. When it does, the white stuff usually doesn't stay around long. You have more to worry about with black-ice on the highway. The only other problem—road wise—is snow on the highways before you reach the coastal stretch.

But don't let a bit of snowy winter weather discourage you from visiting. Watching a storm rage over and in the ocean is awesome, and it will soon be evident where all those drift logs come from.

A word of caution: Going down to the beach at high tide in the winter is NOT RECOMMENDED. Winter tides are much higher than those in the summer, and those drift logs that look light because of the way they bob like corks on the waves—ARE LEATHAL.

20. *Will Rogers*

FEATHERS

If bird watching is your bag, you should be in seventh heaven on the coast, as well as in the forests. Keep your binoculars handy or you'll regret it. To help you find and keep track of the "feathered friends" you'll encounter, besides binoculars, a good bird identifying book is a must. A small pamphlet put out by the *"Northwest Interpretive Association"*[21] will help you keep track and give you an idea of where to look, what to look for by area, where you're most likely to see a particular bird, and when.

The California Gull may be the most common gull you'll see at the seashore. But did you know the California Gull isn't the only gull in these parts? If you're alert and lucky you may just spot a Bonaparte's Gull, Franklin's Gull, Glaucous Gull, Glaucous-winged Gull, Heermann's Gull, Herring Gull, Little Gull, Mew Gull, Ring-billed Gull, Sabine's Gull, Thayer's Gull, or Western Gull. And those are just the "gulls."

There are sandpipers, terns, murrelets, and puffins to be seen. Inland look for hummingbirds, Steller's Jays, crows, ravens and robins, these are some of the more common birds. Rarer sightings may be: Lapland Longspurs, Burrowing owls, peregrine falcons, or an American Coot. Even better, there are a few bald eagles in these parts. The list is endless.

FINS

Some of the sea life you may get lucky enough to see: Dolphins, river otters, sea otters, Dall's porpoise, harbor porpoise, sea lions, harbor seals, gray whales, humpback whales, and killer whales (also called Orca). As with our feathered friends, a good pair of binoculars will give you a definite advantage.

Freshwater fishing within Olympic National Park does NOT require a fishing license unless you're after salmon or steelhead. (There are also a few other exceptions). A fishing license IS required to fish from the ocean shore. Shell fishing requires a license, and you may only use artificial bait. Some areas, as well as some species, are catch and release ONLY. For complete rules and regulations, check the local park service bulletin boards or at the Kalaloch Ranger Station. Ignorance will not save you a fine.

FIRS
RECORD TREES IN OLYMPIC NATIONAL PARK

Olympic National Park is "host" to a fair number of world record trees, in terms of size. The following is a list of those trees recognized by The American Forestry Association as the largest living specimens of the species.

Alaska Cedar

Circumference	Height	Spread
451 inches	124 feet	27 feet

Location: Quinault Sub-District. Approximately 40' north of Big Creek Trail. Approximately 3000 feet elevation.

Grand Fir

Circumference	Height	Spread
229 inches	251 feet	43 feet

Locations: Along the Duckabush River Trail. 7 ½ miles from the trailhead or 1 ½ miles from the park boundary. 100 yards past second stream crossing within park on SE side of the trail.

---

21. *Free at most park service visitor centers, or write to; Northwest Interpretive Assoc.,83 So. King St., suite 212 Seattle Wa.98104*

Subalpine Fir

Circumference	*Height*	*Spread*
252 inches	125 feet	26 feet

Location: About 300 feet east/southeast of Cream Lake which is located at the head of the Hoh River drainage. There is no maintained trail into the area.

Western Hemlock (co-champ)

Circumference	*Height*	*Spread*
270 inches	241 feet	67 feet

Location: Along the Hoh River Trail. 100 yards west of Cougar Creek crossing, 10 yards north of the trail.

Western Hemlock (co-champ)

Circumference	*Height*	*Spread*
291 inches	227 feet	49 feet

Location: On Queets River road 2.8 miles from Matheny Creek, south side of the road.

Western Hemlock (co-champ)

Circumference	*Height*	*Spread*
316 inches	202 feet	47 feet

Location: On ease side of Wynoochee Trail, 1.2 miles from the road's end.

Western Hemlock (co-champ)

Circumference	*Height*	*Spread*
341 inches	174 feet	65 feet

Location: Two miles east of Enchanted Valley Chalet, below rail.

Western Red Cedar

Circumference	*Height*	*Spread*
761 inches	159 feet	45 feet

Location: North Shore of Lake Quinault, across from Rain Forest Motel.

Douglas Fir

Circumference	*Height*	*Spread*
533.5 inches	212 feet	47.5 feet

Largest in Olympic National Park. Not a record tree.
Location: Up Queets River Trail (ford river) 2.4 miles to old Kloochman Rock Trail at Coal Creek; turn left at the junction. The big fir is .2 miles along this trail. There is a sign where you leave the trail and one at the tree. The trail is on the north side of the river.

Douglas Fir

Circumference	*Height*	*Spread*
448 inches	298 feet	64 feet

Largest in Olympic National Park. Not a record tree.
Location: South Fork Hoh River Trail, ¼ mile inside the park boundary, 40' south of the trail.

Sitka Spruce

Circumference	*Height*	*Spread*
707 inches	191 feet	96 feet

Record tree is NOT located in Olympic National Park.
Location: Near Lake Quinault in Olympic National Forest.

Should you be out in the woods some day and just happen to have a tape measure on you, (a long one), and you see a tree bigger than those listed above, contact the American Forest Registry.

LAND MAMMALS

We all owe a debt to the Roosevelt Elk. If it hadn't been for President Roosevelt's desire to maintain the elk herd on the peninsula (even through his intentions were for the purpose of hunting them), Olympic National Park might never have come to be. Instead of a managed forest system and temperate rain forests, the scenery might have become significantly different— as in bald mountains, and tree-stumped clear-cuts.

The Roosevelt Elk is a magnificent animal and a bull elk can weigh up to 1,500 pounds with horns that can spread over five feet. Those horns can weigh fifty pounds without the skull. Needless to say, should you encounter one of these big boys, it's best not to get too close. They don't have the greatest sense of humor in the world, and those antlers could make you a shish kabob in short order, especially during the mating season.

A few other mammals you may encounter in the park:

Black Bear	Beaver	Bobcat
Chipmunk (Olympic)	Chipmunk (Townsend's)	Cougar
Coyote	Deer (Black-tailed)	Red Fox
Marmot (Olympic)	Marten	Mink
Muskrat	River Otter	Porcupine
Raccoon	Skunk (spotted)	Skunk (striped)
Snowshoe Hare	Squirrel (Douglas)	Squirrel (northern
Weasel (short-tailed)	Weasel (long-tailed)	flying)

A few words of caution are also due here about cougars, and black bears.

Cougars. These large cats are extremely reclusive and chances are you'll never encounter one. On the other hand, it is best to be prepared. Should you see a cougar, it will most likely flee as quickly as possible, as long as it has an escape route. DON'T EVER CORNER ONE.

Should you come around that next corner and come face-to-face with a feline, the best things to do are: Back up if possible. DO NOT TURN AND RUN. You can't out run it. If you have small children with you, pick them up. Sometimes the appearance of something LARGER will do the trick.

The other large mammal that you may encounter when out tramping in the woods is the black-bear, *ursus americanus*. While it's also highly unlikely you'll ever see a bear, knowing how to react could just literally save your bacon. If you happen upon a black bear while driving, STAY IN YOUR CAR. Getting out there for a "close-up" with the old camera is not an intelligent decision. If you don't have 357 horses under you, it's best to make some noise while hiking. If they hear you coming, most bears will avoid you like the plague. But, should you be unlucky enough to end up between a mother and her cubs, pal, you're in a lot of trouble.

Unlike a grizzly bear, "playing dead" is not generally a good idea. Black bears, usually, don't go for the "broken-wing" act. Climbing a tree isn't going to work either. The bear can climb faster than you can anyway. If you have food in a backpack, drop the pack and BACK AWAY. DO NOT RUN. Better to lose a $200 backpack than your life If the bear is distracted enough with the opportunity for food, and you can back up far enough to get out of sight, and while bruno's busy shredding your pack, then you can run like hell. If this doesn't work, your only hope is that you can run faster than your hiking partner.

These bear and cougar stories aren't told to keep you out of the woods. By all means go. Enjoy yourself. Hike and trek and tramp until you can't take another step. But, it's a foolish "backwoodsperson" who isn't prepared for those little unexpected things that can happen.

Another seemingly harmless creature, and one that for some reason everyone seems to think it's okay to feed tidbits to, is the raccoon. These darling little balls of fur easily adjust to human handouts. In fact, they even seem to perform for that cracker or piece of bread you're holding for them. Sure. They'll even take food right out of your hand. "Ooooh, aren't they just the cutest things? And so tame." Yes, they are cute. NO they are not tame.

If you'd like to see a whole new meaning to the word chutzpa, wait till you see what happens when you run out of food and the raccoon hasn't run out of "hungry." Stick an empty hand out there and you'll most likely get bit. Then, just for kicks, when you call a ranger to complain about this *ferocious beast* that, "Just came out of nowhere and bit me," Mr. Ranger can give you a fine, and you'll end up having rabies shots. Ever had a rabies shot? Neither have I. From what I understand though, they hurt—a lot!

Basically, whether it is a mountain lion or a ground squirrel, leave the four-legged critters alone. The things we humans eat are NOT creature-friendly. Have you ever seen a bird with its talons curled up so tightly it can't walk or perch on a tree limb? Potato chips and popcorn will do that. The sodium and oils in human food is meant for "our" digestive systems—not theirs.

Overall, everyone of us at Kalaloch, lodge employees, park service people, and campground hosts, hope you have the time of your life while visiting us. And remember, take nothing but pictures, leave nothing but footprints, and we'll see you soon.

91. Which of the following is *not* a key concept of the Gestalt group?
    a. awareness
    b. unfinished business
    c. understanding one's irrational beliefs
    d. here-and-now focus
    e. dealing with the impasse

92. The founder of transactional analysis is
    a. Robert Goulding.
    b. Eric Berne.
    c. J. L. Moreno.
    d. William Glasser.
    e. Albert Bandura.

93. Which of the following techniques is not considered a behavioral technique?
    a. self-instruction
    b. the dialogue technique
    c. cognitive restructuring
    d. self-reinforcement
    e. coaching

94. REBT methodology includes all of the following procedures except
    a. confrontation.
    b. logical analysis.
    c. analysis of one's life script.
    d. counterpropaganda.
    e. behavioral methods.

95. Which of the following is not a key concept of reality therapy?
    a. Members must make commitments.
    b. Members focus on early childhood issues.
    c. Members make an evaluation of their behavior.
    d. Members focus on the present, not the past.
    e. Members look at ways in which they are choosing their total behavior.

96. In an analytic group, free association might be used for
    a. working on dreams.
    b. encouraging spontaneity among members.
    c. promoting interaction between members.
    d. getting at unconscious material.
    e. all of the above.

97. All of the following are key concepts underlying the Adlerian group except for one.
    a. teleology
    b. social interest
    c. creativity and choice
    d. developing a lifestyle
    e. A-B-C theory of personality

98. Which of the following techniques is least likely to be used in psychodrama?
    a. script analysis
    b. doubling
    c. future projection
    d. role reversal
    e. soliloquy

_____ 99. In an existential group, which technique would be considered essential?
  a. role playing
  b. rational-emotive imagery
  c. homework
  d. dream analysis
  e. none of the above

_____ 100. The term that best captures the role and functions of a person-centered group counselor is
  a. teacher.
  b. facilitator.
  c. expert.
  d. companion.

_____ 101. Which of the following is generally *not* a technique used in Gestalt groups?
  a. experiments with dialogues
  b. making the rounds
  c. teaching rational thinking
  d. working with dreams
  e. focusing on nonverbal communication

_____ 102. Which of the following is *not* a key concept of TA groups?
  a. lifestyle assessment
  b. analysis of ego states
  c. strokes
  d. script analysis
  e. games

_____ 103. During the initial stage of a behavioral group the concern of the group leader is
  a. to identify problematic behavior.
  b. to develop baseline data.
  c. to teach members about the group process.
  d. to conduct an assessment of each member's current behavior.
  e. to do all of the above.

_____ 104. In an REBT group, role playing involves
  a. a catharsis.
  b. a cognitive restructuring of beliefs.
  c. a return to some event during early childhood.
  d. promoting an expression of feelings between members.
  e. none of the above.

_____ 105. Which of the following is a typical procedure used in reality-therapy groups?
  a. conducting an assessment of one's family constellation
  b. exploring early childhood experiences
  c. fostering transference reactions toward the leader
  d. analyzing ego states
  e. evaluating current behavior

_____ 106. Dreams are explored in
  a. Gestalt groups.
  b. psychoanalytic groups.

c. psychodrama groups.

d. Adlerian groups.

e. all of the above.

_____ 107. The object-relations theory is associated with

a. behavior therapy.

b. Gestalt therapy.

c. Adlerian therapy.

d. reality therapy.

e. none of the above.

_____ 108. Creativity and choice are stressed in

a. Adlerian therapy.

b. existential therapy.

c. reality therapy.

d. Gestalt therapy.

e. all of the above.

_____ 109. Insight is stressed in all of the approaches *except* for one.

a. psychoanalytic therapy

b. psychodrama

c. reality therapy

d. Gestalt therapy

e. TA

_____ 110. The process of skillful questioning would be used mostly by a group leader with which theoretical orientation?

a. person-centered therapy

b. reality therapy

c. Gestalt therapy

d. existential therapy

e. none of the above

_____ 111. Unfinished business and avoidance are key concepts of

a. Gestalt therapy.

b. reality therapy.

c. behavior therapy.

d. rational emotive behavior therapy.

e. none of the above.

_____ 112. Which type of group serves the function of re-creating the original family, so that members can work through their unresolved problems?

a. REBT

b. behavioral

c. psychoanalytic

d. TA

e. person-centered

_____ 113. Individual Psychology is another name for

a. psychoanalytic therapy.

b. Adlerian therapy.

c. existential therapy.

d. reality therapy.
e. person-centered therapy.

_____ 114. Contracts and homework assignments are most likely to be used in
a. TA groups.
b. behavior-therapy groups.
c. reality-therapy groups.
d. REBT groups.
e. all of the above.

_____ 115. Which approach would be least interested in the exploration of early childhood experiences?
a. reality therapy
b. psychoanalytic therapy
c. Gestalt therapy
d. Adlerian therapy
e. TA

_____ 116. A basic premise that we are not the victims of circumstances because we choose our behavior is emphasized in
a. existential therapy.
b. reality therapy.
c. person-centered therapy.
d. TA.
e. all of the above.

_____ 117. Concepts of introjection, projection, retroflection, confluence, and deflection are part of
a. Adlerian therapy.
b. psychodrama.
c. Gestalt therapy.
d. existential therapy.
e. TA.

_____ 118. The concept of basic psychological life positions is part of
a. psychoanalytic therapy.
b. TA.
c. psychodrama.
d. REBT.
e. none of the above.

_____ 119. Which theory would be most concerned with understanding and exploring an individual's developmental stages?
a. TA
b. psychoanalytic therapy
c. behavior therapy
d. REBT
e. none of the above

_____ 120. The socioteleological approach that holds that people are primarily motivated by social forces and striving to achieve certain goals is
a. person-centered therapy.
b. existential therapy.
c. reality therapy.

198

d. Adlerian therapy.

e. behavior therapy.

_____ 121. Which type of group counselor would tend to provide the least degree of direction?

a. REBT therapist

b. person-centered therapist

c. Gestalt therapist

d. reality therapist

e. behavior therapist

_____ 122. The here and now is emphasized in

a. psychodrama.

b. existential therapy.

c. person-centered therapy.

d. Gestalt therapy.

e. all of the above.

_____ 123. Multimodal group therapy is associated with which theoretical approach?

a. behavior therapy

b. TA

c. reality therapy

d. Adlerian therapy

e. existential therapy

_____ 124. The A-B-C theory is associated with

a. reality therapy.

b. TA.

c. behavior therapy.

d. REBT.

e. Gestalt therapy.

_____ 125. A focus on ego states would occur in

a. Gestalt groups.

b. Adlerian groups.

c. TA groups.

d. psychodrama groups.

e. all of the above.

_____ 126. Which approach most relies on empirical research to validate its techniques?

a. reality therapy

b. behavior therapy

c. person-centered therapy

d. existential therapy

e. TA

_____ 127. Cognitive homework is likely to be assigned in

a. psychodrama groups.

b. psychoanalytic groups.

c. REBT groups.

d. reality-therapy groups.

e. Gestalt groups.

_____ 128. Modeling would be important in which type of group?

a. reality therapy

b. behavior therapy
c. REBT
d. existential therapy
e. all of the above

_____ 129. Control theory is a basic part of the practice of
a. behavior therapy.
b. REBT.
c. reality therapy.
d. Adlerian therapy.
e. existential therapy.

_____ 130. The role of the family would be stressed mostly in which type of group?
a. psychodrama
b. behavioral
c. existential
d. Gestalt
e. Adlerian

_____ 131. Injunctions, early decisions, and redecisions are key concepts stressed in which type of group?
a. Adlerian
b. TA
c. Gestalt
d. REBT
e. reality therapy

_____ 132. Which approach would be most likely to focus on an expression and exploration of feelings?
a. behavior therapy
b. REBT
c. reality therapy
d. Gestalt therapy
e. none of the above

_____ 133. Significant developments in dealing with borderline and narcissistic personality disorders have occurred within which theory?
a. Gestalt therapy
b. TA
c. behavior therapy
d. person-centered therapy
e. none of the above

_____ 134. Dealing with the present is stressed in
a. psychodrama.
b. Gestalt therapy.
c. existential therapy.
d. reality therapy.
e. all of the above.

_____ 135. Which approach does not emphasize techniques?
a. Adlerian therapy
b. psychodrama
c. existential therapy

d. behavior therapy

e. REBT

___ 136. Which theory focuses on cognition?

a. Adlerian

b. Gestalt

c. REBT

d. psychodrama

e. two of the above

___ 137. Success identity and positive addiction are basic concepts in

a. TA.

b. existential therapy.

c. REBT.

d. reality therapy.

e. Gestalt therapy.

___ 138. A lifestyle investigation, which would focus on family background and would reveal a pattern of basic mistakes, would be used in

a. psychoanalytic therapy.

b. Adlerian therapy.

c. behavior therapy.

d. REBT.

e. all of the above.

___ 139. Which type of group leader is most likely to focus on energy and blocks to energy?

a. Adlerian

b. Gestalt

c. psychoanalytic

d. TA

e. person-centered

___ 140. The therapeutic conditions of congruence, unconditional positive regard, and empathy are emphasized in

a. psychoanalytic therapy.

b. reality therapy.

c. TA.

d. person-centered therapy.

e. none of the above.

___ 141. Role playing is likely to be used in

a. psychodrama.

b. Gestalt therapy.

c. REBT.

d. behavior therapy.

e. all of the above.

___ 142. The approach that stresses the total behavior of doing, thinking, feeling, and physiology is

a. REBT.

b. reality therapy.

c. person-centered therapy.

d. psychoanalytic therapy.

e. TA.

_____ 143. Which approach emphasizes the personal qualities of the group leader rather than the techniques of leading?
   a. existential
   b. person-centered
   c. REBT
   d. behavioral
   e. two of the above

_____ 144. The approach that teaches members how to identify irrational beliefs and substitute rational beliefs is
   a. reality therapy.
   b. REBT.
   c. TA.
   d. Gestalt therapy.
   e. behavior therapy.

_____ 145. Social-skill-training groups most rely on which type of techniques?
   a. behavioral
   b. TA
   c. psychodramatic
   d. reality therapy
   e. Adlerian

_____ 146. In which type of group would members focus on their life scripts through the process of script analysis?
   a. psychoanalytic
   b. reality therapy
   c. behavioral
   d. Adlerian
   e. none of the above

_____ 147. Shame-attacking exercises are likely to be used in which type of group?
   a. reality therapy
   b. person-centered
   c. Gestalt
   d. REBT
   e. psychodrama

_____ 148. Which theoretical approach would most contribute to teaching members coping skills to manage stress?
   a. person-centered therapy
   b. reality therapy
   c. Adlerian therapy
   d. behavior therapy
   e. Gestalt therapy

_____ 149. The group leader assumes the role of a teacher in which approach?
   a. TA
   b. reality therapy
   c. behavior therapy
   d. REBT
   e. all of the above

_____ 150. Which approach has the goal of uncovering unconscious conflicts and working them through?
   a. person-centered therapy
   b. reality therapy
   c. psychoanalytic therapy
   d. TA
   e. behavior therapy

Essay Questions for Review and Study

Directions: These questions are designed as a study guide to help you pull together some central ideas in the textbook. Strive to write your answers briefly, using your own words.

1. What are the values of a group for special populations (children, adolescents, or adults)?

2. Differentiate between
   a. group psychotherapy and group counseling.
   b. group psychotherapy and self-help groups.

3. If you were working in a setting with clients representing diverse cultural backgrounds, what would you see as your major challenge as a group leader? How might you meet some of these challenges?

4. What do you see as a few of the advantages and disadvantages of group counseling with ethnic and minority clients?

5. What are some guidelines that could help you design and conduct groups with culturally diverse populations?

6. See Chapter 2 of this manual, and review the inventories that you filled out on ethical issues in group work. Have you changed your thinking from the beginning to the end of the course on any of these ethical issues?

7. Review the ASGW's ethical guidelines, and select one on which you would most like to comment.

8. Assume that you are a counselor in a community agency. No groups are being offered, and you see a need for several types of groups. What course of action, if any, might you be inclined to take?

9. When you think of conducting groups, what minimal training and preparation would you want?

10. Review the section in Chapter 3 that deals with the group leader as a person. What are your major personal characteristics that would help you and hinder you in your work as a group leader?

11. In the same chapter, review the section dealing with special problems and issues for beginning group leaders. Discuss your single most important concern.

12. Assume that you are working in an agency and would like to form a group. The director would like you to co-lead your groups. What specific things would you look for in selecting a co-leader?

13. Discuss what you see as your major tasks at each of the stages in the development of a group.

14. Assume that you were in a job interview and were asked this question: "Tell us about the theoretical orientation that guides your practice as a group counselor." How would you answer?

15. There are different styles of group leadership. Again, in a job interview, how might you describe your own personal style of leadership?

16. Think of a particular group that you might conduct, and describe briefly what factors you would consider in forming it.

17. The stages of a group do not generally flow neatly and predictably in the order described in the textbook. Why is it important that you have a clear understanding of the characteristics associated with the development of a group?

18. If you had to select the one theory that comes closest to your thinking and that helps you in your practice as a group counselor, which would it be? Explain the reasons for your selection.

19. Contrast a psychoanalytic group with a reality-therapy group in terms of goals and procedures used.

20. Dreams can be fruitfully explored by using several different therapy approaches. Show how you might work with a dream in a group format from these three perspectives: psychoanalytic, psychodrama, and Gestalt.

21. Compare the goals of psychodrama and Gestalt groups; contrast the differences in techniques between these two approaches.

22. Discuss some common denominators of these various approaches to group counseling: Adlerian therapy, TA, REBT, reality therapy.

23. In what ways does reality therapy draw on both the existential and behavioral approaches?

24. Select one of the following possible combinations and discuss what you see as being some of the merits of merging the concepts and techniques of the two approaches as applied to group counseling: Gestalt with TA, Gestalt with REBT, or Gestalt with reality therapy.

25. Assume that you are leading a group with culturally diverse members. Are there any concepts and techniques from the various approaches that you would find particularly useful?

26. Discuss some of the ways of combining existential themes with behavioral techniques. What are the possibilities of a merger between the existential and behavioral approaches as applied to group counseling?

27. What are some commonalities between a person-centered group and an existential group? What are some basic differences?

28. How would you describe your role as a group counselor to a new group? What do you see as your major leadership functions?

29. How would you assess the outcomes of a group that you were leading?

30. Discuss the role that theory plays in the practice of group counseling. How does the theory that a leader holds influence the interventions he or she makes?

◆ APPENDIX I ◆

Scoring Key
for Chapter Quizzes

ITEM NO.	PSYCHOANALYTIC CH. 6	ADLERIAN CH. 7	PSYCHODRAMA CH. 8	EXISTENTIAL CH. 9	PERSON-CENTERED CH. 10	GESTALT CH. 11	TA CH. 12	BEHAVIOR THERAPY CH. 13	REBT CH. 14	REALITY THERAPY CH. 15	ITEM NO.
1.	F	T	T	F	T	F	F	T	T	T	1.
2.	T	T	F	T	T	T	F	F	F	T	2.
3.	F	T	F	T	T	F	T	F	T	T	3.
4.	F	F	T	F	F	F	F	T	T	F	4.
5.	F	T	T	T	F	T	T	F	T	F	5.
6.	T	F	F	F	T	T	T	T	F	T	6.
7.	F	F	F	F	F	F	T	T	F	F	7.
8.	T	F	T	F	T	F	T	T	T	T	8.
9.	T	T	F	T	F	T	F	F	T	F	9.
10.	T	T	F	F	T	T	T	T	T	T	10.
11.	a	b	a	b	d	e	d	d	c	b	11.
12.	b	e	d	c	b	c	e	b	a	a	12.
13.	e	a	b	c	e	a	b	a	c	d	13.
14.	c	e	c	b	e	d	d	c	a	a	14.
15.	e	c	b	d	b	e	d	d	e	b	15.
16.	c	b	c	b	b	c	c	c	d	b	16.
17.	e	d	e	b	a	e	b	d	e	d	17.
18.	a	c	e	c	b	a	d	e	d	d	18.
19.	c	d	c	a	a	b	e	e	a	a	19.
20.	b	b	e	a	c	b	a	d	c	b	20.

207

Answer Key for Comprehension Check and General Test

1. c	2. d	3. a	4. d	5. b	6. e	7. b
8. a	9. c	10. e	11. b	12. c	13. e	14. b
15. e	16. b	17. b	18. e	19. c	20. e	21. c
22. b	23. a	24. c	25. b	26. a	27. b	28. e
29. a	30. b	31. F	32. T	33. T	34. F	35. T
36. F	37. T	38. T	39. T	40. F	41. F	42. F
43. T	44. F	45. F	46. F	47. T	48. T	49. F
50. F	51. b	52. e	53. c	54. a	55. a	56. d
57. b	58. e	59. b	60. d	61. c	62. c	63. c
64. a	65. a	66. b	67. d	68. c	69. d	70. a
71. b	72. a	73. e	74. b	75. d	76. c	77. b
78. e	79. a	80. d	81. c	82. e	83. e	84. a
85. a	86. a	87. b	88. c	89. d	90. c	91. c
92. b	93. b	94. c	95. b	96. e	97. e	98. a
99. e	100. b	101. c	102. a	103. e	104. b	105. e
106. e	107. e	108. e	109. c	110. b	111. a	112. c

113. b	114. e	115. a	116. e	117. c	118. b	119. b
120. d	121. b	122. e	123. a	124. d	125. c	126. b
127. c	128. e	129. c	130. e	131. b	132. d	133. e
134. e	135. c	136. e	137. d	138. b	139. b	140. d
141. e	142. b	143. e	144. b	145. a	146. e	147. d
148. d	149. e	150. c				

◆ APPENDIX III ◆

Other Books by the Author

The following are other books that my colleagues and I have authored or co-authored that might be of interest to you. All of these are published by the Brooks/Cole Publishing Company, Pacific Grove, CA 93950.

Corey, G. (1991). *Theory and Practice of Counseling and Psychotherapy,* 4th ed. Presents an overview of nine contemporary theories of counseling, with an emphasis on the practical applications and the therapeutic process associated with each orientation.

Corey, G. (1991). *Manual for Theory and Practice of Counseling and Psychotherapy,* 4th ed. Similar to the present manual.

Corey, G. (1991). *Case Approach to Counseling and Psychotherapy,* 3rd ed. Designed to demonstrate how theory can be applied to specific cases. Outline of theories corresponds to your textbook and manual (with the exception of psychodrama). Readers are challenged to apply their knowledge of theories to a variety of cases. I demonstrate my way of working with these cases from each of nine theoretical perspectives and also in an eclectic, integrated fashion. Also, for each of the nine theories there is a central case (Ruth). A proponent of each theory writes about his or her assessment of Ruth and then proceeds to demonstrate his or her particular therapeutic style in counseling Ruth. I then follow up and show how I might intervene with Ruth by staying within the general framework of each of these theories.

Corey, M. S., & Corey, G. (1992). *Groups: Process and Practice,* 4th ed. Outlines the basic issues and concepts of group process throughout the life history of a group. Applies these basic concepts to groups for children, adolescents, adults, and the elderly.

Corey, G., Corey, M. S., Callanan, P., & Russell, J. M. (1992). *Group Techniques,* 2nd ed. Describes ideas for creating and implementing techniques for use in groups. Gives a rationale for the use of techniques in all the stages in a group's development.

Corey, G., & Corey, M. S. (1993). *I Never Knew I Had a Choice,* 5th ed. A self-help book for personal growth that deals with topics such as the struggle to achieve autonomy; the roles that work, sex roles, sexuality, love, intimacy, and solitude play in our lives; the meaning of loneliness, death, and loss; and the ways in which we choose values and find meaning in life.

Corey, M. S., & Corey, G. (1993). *Becoming a Helper,* 2nd ed. This book deals with topics of concern to students who are studying in one of the helping professions. Some of the issues explored are examining your motivations and needs, becoming aware of the impact of your values on the counseling process, learning to cope with stress, dealing with burnout, exploring developmental turning points in one's life, and ethical issues.

Corey, G., Corey, M. S., & Callanan, P. (1993). *Issues and Ethics in the Helping Professions,* 4th ed. A combination textbook and student manual that contains self-inventories, open-ended cases and problem situations, exercises, suggested activities, and a variety of ethical, professional, and legal issues facing practitioners.

TO THE OWNER OF THIS BOOK:

I hope that you have enjoyed the *Student Manual for Theory and Practice of Group Counseling* (fourth edition). I'd like to know as much about your experiences with the manual as possible. Only through your comments and the comments of others can I learn how to make the manual a better book for future readers.

School: _____ Instructor's name: _____

Name of course: _____

1. What I like *most* about this manual is: _____

_____

_____

2. What I like *least* about this manual is: _____

_____

_____

3. My specific suggestions for improving the manual are: _____

_____

_____

4. Some ways in which I used this manual in class were: _____

_____

5. Some ways in which I used this manual out of class were: _____

_____

6. Some of the manual's exercises that were used most meaningfully in my class were:

_____

_____

7. My general reaction to this manual is: _____

_____

8. In the space below, or in a separate letter, please write any other comments about the book you'd like to make. I welcome your suggestions!

Optional:

Your name: _____ Date: _____

May Brooks/Cole quote you, either in promotion for the *Student Manual for Theory and Practice of Group Counseling* or in future publishing ventures?

Yes: _____ No: _____

Sincerely,

Gerald Corey

Brooks/Cole Publishing is dedicated to publishing quality publications for the helping professions. If you would like to learn more about our publications, please use this mailer to request our catalogue.

Name: _____

Address: _____

City/State/Zip code: _____

FOLD HERE

NO POSTAGE
NECESSARY
IF MAILED
IN THE
UNITED STATES

FOLD HERE